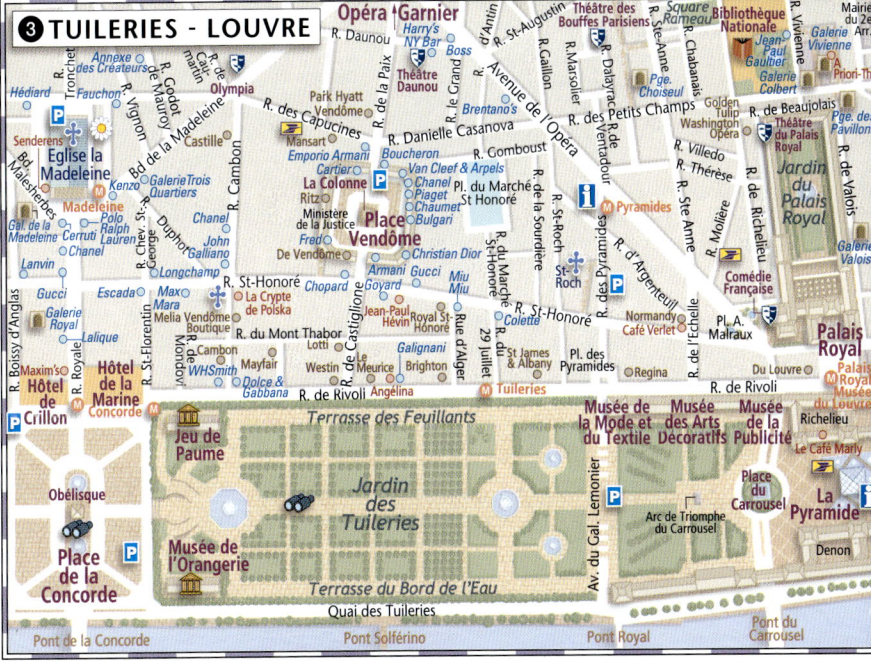

index

A
- Airports **46–47**
- Annual Events **59–60**
- Arc de Triomphe **5**
- ATMs **51**

B
- Banks **51**
- Bars **40–42**
- Boat Tours **53**
- Bois de Boulogne **6**
- Book Shops **20**
- Brasseries **40–42**
- Bureaux de Change **52**
- Bus Tours **53**
- Buses **46, 47–48**

C
- Cabaret **26–27**
- Cafés **42–43**
- Canal Tours **53**
- Car Hire **49**
- Cinema **27–28**
- Classical Music **30–31**
- Climate **49–50**
- Clubs **28–29**
- Coaches **47**
- Credit Cards **51**
- Cycle Hire **49–50**
- Cycling **31**

D
- Department Stores **17–18**
- Directory **54–61**
- Disabled Access **50**
- Dome Church **7**
- Driving **49**

E
- Electricity **50**
- Embassies **51, 50**
- Emergencies **53**
- Entertainment **24–31**

F
- Folies Bergère **27**
- Food & Drink Shops **22–23**
- Football **31**

G
- Grand Palais **6–7**
- Grande Arche **6**

H
- Horse Racing **31**
- Hôtel des Invalides **7**
- Hotels **54–57**

I
- Ile de la Cité **7**
- Ile St-Louis **7**
- Internet Cafés **51**

J
- Jardin du Luxembourg **8**
- Jardin du Palais-Royal **8**
- Jardin des Tuileries **9**
- Jazz **29**

K
- Kids' Venues **59**

L
- La Défense **6**
- Latin Quarter **4, 16**
- Lost Property **51**

M
- Mail **52**
- Markets **18–20**
- Medical Care **51, 52**
- Metro **47–48**
- Money **39, 51–52, 53**
- Montmartre **4**
- Montparnasse **4–5**
- Moulin Rouge **27**
- Museums **9–10, 57–58**
- Museum Pass **5**
- Musée Carnavalet **9**
- Musée du Louvre **9**
- Musée National du Moyen Age **9**
- Musée d'Orsay **9–10**
- Musée Picasso **10**
- Musée du Quai Branly **10**
- Musée Rodin **10**

N
- Newspapers **61**
- Notre-Dame **10**

O
- Opera **29–30**

P
- Palais de Chaillot **11**
- Panthéon **11**
- Parks & Gardens **8–9, 58–59**
- Petit Palais **11–12**
- Pharmacies **52**
- Place de la Bastille **12**
- Place de la Concorde **12**
- Place Vendôme **12**
- Pompidou Centre **12**
- Public Holidays **52–53**

R
- RATP **47–48**
- Restaurants **34–40**
- RER **46, 47–48**
- River Tours **53**
- Rugby **31**

S
- Sacré Coeur **12–13**
- Safety **52**
- Sainte-Chapelle **13**
- Shopping **14–23**
- Sights **2–13, 57–58**
- Sorbonne **13**
- Sport **31**

T
- Taxis **46–47, 49**
- Telephones **53**
- Tennis **31**
- Theatre **26, 48**
- Tickets **26, 48**
- Tipping **39, 53**
- Tour Eiffel **13**
- Tourist Information **46**
- Tours **53**
- Trains **46, 47–48**
- Transport **46–50**

W
- Websites **61**

Whilst every care has been taken to check the accuracy of the information in this guide, the publishers cannot accept responsibility for errors or omissions or the consequences thereof. No part of this guide may be reproduced without the permission of the publishers. Published by Compass Maps Ltd.
info@popoutmaps.com
www.popout-travel.com
© 2009 Compass Maps Ltd. All rights reserved.

Written by Robert George, Garry Marchant, Sophie Vernay, Fiona Quinn and Helen Baker.
All pictures © Compass Maps Ltd and John Heseltine except the following courtesy of Paris Tourist Board: p.4, p.10, p.31, p.40, p.41, p.43, p.47, p.48, p.50 Amélie Dupont, p.8, p.30 David Lefranc, p.12 Henri Garat, p.39 Mark Bertrand; the following courtesy of Shutterstock: p.6L, p.11, Joaquin Alfonso Perez; p.6R Grace Victoria, p.7L Elena Elisseeva, p.26 Rachelle Burnside; p.3 Alamy/EJ Images; p.7R, p.48 GettyImages/Photodisc; p.15 Alamy/John Norman; p.18, p.19 Susannah Sayler; p.25 Alamy/Ian Shaw; p32-33 Getty/Martial Clomb; p.35 Alamy/Sandra Baker; p.38R Giles Philippot; p.45 Alamy/Ron Chapple; p.49 Sophie Robichon/Mairie de Paris.
Cover Images: Ekaterina Krasnikova/Shutterstock and Travel Pix Ltd/PCL.
This PopOut insideout product, its associated machinery and format use, whether singular or integrated within other products, is subject to worldwide patents granted & pending, including EP1417665, CN ZL02819864.6 & CN ZL200620006638.7. All rights reserved including design, copyright, trademark and associated intellectual property rights. PopOut is a registered trademark and is produced under license by CompassMaps Ltd.

7941

speak it

Some people in Paris are fluent in English and occasionally you will find someone who will brush aside your French and respond in faultless English, or simply pretend not to understand you. Most people, however, will appreciate your efforts to speak the lingo.

Useful phrases

hello – **bonjour**
goodbye – **au revoir**
hello/goodbye – **salut**
today – **aujourd'hui**
yesterday – **hier**
tomorrow – **demain**
yes – **oui**
no – **non**
please – **s'il vous plaît**
thank you – **merci**
now – **maintenant**
later – **plus tard**
open – **ouvert**
closed – **fermé**
a little – **un peu**
a lot – **beaucoup**
expensive – **cher**
inexpensive – **pas cher**
where – **où**
when – **quand**
why – **pourquoi**
right – **droit**
straight ahead – **tout droit**
left – **gauche**
big – **grand**
small – **petit**
good – **bien**
bad – **mauvais**
help me – **aidez-moi**
airmail – **par avion**
credit card – **la carte de credit**
will you? – **voulez-vous?**
how much? – **c'est combien?**
post office – **le bureau de poste**

Numbers

0 – **zero**, 1 – **un**, 2 – **deux**, 3 – **trois**, 4 – **quatre**, 5 – **cinq**, 6 – **six**, 7 – **sept**, 8 – **huit**, 9 – **neuf**, 10 – **dix**, 20 – **vingt**, 30 – **trente**, 100 – **cent**, 1,000 – **mille**

Days of the week

Monday – **lundi**
Tuesday – **mardi**
Wednesday – **mercredi**
Thursday – **jeudi**
Friday – **vendredi**
Saturday – **samedi**
Sunday – **dimanche**

In the restaurant

breakfast – **le petit déjeuner**
lunch – **le déjeuner**
dinner – **le dîner**
menu – **la carte**
bread – **le pain**
coffee – **le café**
tea – **le thé**
butter – **le beurre**
water – **l'eau**
milk – **le lait**
beer – **la bière**
wine – **le vin**
soup – **la soupe**
meat – **la viande**
ham – **le jambon**
fish – **le poisson**
chicken – **le poulet**
salt – **le sel**
pepper – **le poivre**
bill – **l'addition**
cup – **la tasse**
glass – **le verre**
eggs – **les oeufs**

Fête du Beaujolais Nouveau:
A good excuse to visit a café or wine bar to celebrate the new vintage (third Thurs).

December

Noël:
Christmas Eve is celebrated with midnight mass held at both Cathédrale Notre-Dame *(see p.10)* and Eglise de la Madeleine.

Listings

There are, unfortunately, few publications with English information on events and venues, although there are many in French. Check out these below:

FUSAC
FUSAC (France-USA Contacts), an English-speaking free biweekly with extensive classified ads for housing, jobs, schools etc. It is especially useful for long stayers. www.fusac.fr

Le Figaro
Leading French morning paper. The listings section comes out on Wednesday.

Le Monde
Daily newspaper's listings section; comes out on Wednesday.

Pariscope and Officiel des Spectacles
These two inexpensive, pocket-sized publications with extensive listings (only in French) come out every Wednesday. Thorough, and very helpful if you can work out the system. Pariscope has the more extensive listings out of the two.

Where
This free monthly publication has useful information on everything from arts and antiques to dining and entertainment.

Newspapers

Overseas English-language newspapers are available at many news kiosks and *tabacs* (tobacconists) tourist areas.

The International Herald Tribune
This historic daily international newspaper published in Paris in English is the best source for international news, sports and business information. It also has strong cultural coverage, with listings of important events worldwide, especially in Europe. www.iht.com

Irish Eyes
This monthly runs articles in English and French on art, music and books as well as interviews, news and reviews of interest to the anglophone community. www.irisheyes.fr

Le Figaro
Serious daily. www.lefigaro.fr
Le Monde
Highbrow daily. www.lemonde.fr
Libération
Founded by J-P Sartre. Left wing. www.liberation.fr

Websites

www.parisinfo.com
Official website of the Paris Convention & Visitors Bureau.
www.paris.org Travel listings site.
www.timeout.com/paris
Travel guide listings site.
www.parisvoice.com
Webzine for English-speaking Parisians.
www.pagesjaunes.fr
French yellow pages online.

May

Fête du Travail (May Day):
With everything closed people take to the streets to celebrate the public holiday with festivals and marches. Expect to see Lilies of the valley (*muguet*) on sale citywide.

Shakespeare Garden Festival:
Bois de Boulogne (*see p.6*), outdoor plays from May-October.

Musique Cité Jardin:
Music is performed in the city's parks and gardens from May to October.

French Tennis Open Championship: Stade Roland-Garros from late May-early June (*see p.31*).

June

Fête de la Musique:
A night of concerts all over the city (21 June).

Gay Pride March:
Camp and colourful parade towards the Bastille (28 June).

Paris Air Show:
Le Bourget Airport (mid June). www.salon-du-bourget.fr

Prix de Diane Hermès:
Chantilly. Ascot-style event at the races (2nd Sun).

Paris Jazz Festival:
Offering the best in jazz, the festival plays from early June to the end of July. *Parc Floral de Paris, www.parcfloraldeparis.com*

July

Paris Plage:
Every summer, from mid-July to mid-August, the city creates a 'beach' along 3 km (1.8 miles) of the Seine (❷ 3E-5H), complete with palm trees, swimming pools, and sand.

Bastille Day:
The whole of Paris parties to celebrate the anniversary of French independence. Fireworks (14th).

Tour de France:
Ends in the Champs-Elysées. Mid-month after a three-week voyage round the country.

August

Festival Cinéma au Clair de Lune (Open-air Cinema): Complete with a giant outdoor screen, film favourites and a party atmosphere. *http://clairdelune.forumdesimages.net*

September

Journée de Patrimoine:
Historic monuments and museums open to the public for free over two days (3rd weekend).

Paris Autumn Festival:
Celebrates autumnal events from mid-September to the end of December. www.festival-automne.com

October

Nuit Blanche (Sleepless Night):
All night (first or second Sat) you can visit the normally hidden side of Paris, revealed through performances, monument visits and installations.

Prix de l'Arc de Triomphe:
Flash day's racing at Longchamp (first week *see p.31*).

November

Paris Tennis Open:
Palais Omnisports de Paris-Bercy (❶ 6H).

dens lining its arcades. Its garden is now a peaceful place for a quiet wander. Check out the Cours d'Honneur and the 280 black and white humbug-stick like columns sculpted by Daniel Buren.

Kids' Paris

There are many child-friendly hotels offering family rooms.

Many museums also offer reductions in price or free entry for under-18s.

It is best to avoid busy restaurants at peak times with very young children or toddlers; high chairs and baby seats are not often provided and there's generally not much room for letting off steam.

Cinéaqua ❶ 3C/❷ 3A

Paris's latest aquarium boasts the largest tank in France at 33 metres long. Kids will love the 'Touch Pool' where they can feel the trusting Koï fish and other sturgeon. *5 Avenue Albert De Mun, T: 01 40 69 23 23, www.cineaqua.com*

La Croisière Enchantée ❷ 3B

Bateaux Parisiens (see p.53) offer an enchanted boat trip up the river Seine at the weekend and during school holidays (approximately one hour). Suits the under-tens. *Port de la Bourdonnais, T: 01 76 64 14 45, www.bateauxparisiens.com*

Galerie des Enfants ❷ 3H/❹

Well-presented exhibitions by major artists give children a taste of modern art. *Centre Pompidou (see p.6), T: 01 44 78 12 33 www.centrepompidou.fr*

La Ménagerie ❷ 6H

Old-fashioned zoo (one of the oldest), within the Jardins des Plantes but good entertainment for the younger children. *Jardins des Plantes, 57 rue Cuvier, T: 01 40 79 37 94, www.mnhn.fr*

Parc Zoölogique de Paris

A well-landscaped zoo park where the inhabitants do get some degree of freedom. *53 avenue de St-Maurice, Bois de Vincennes, T: 01 44 75 20 00, www.mnhn.fr*

Playgrounds & Playtime

There are playgrounds in most major parks and there is a boating lake in the Jardin du Luxembourg (see p.8) where children can hire model sailing-boats, and watch a puppet theatre.

Annual Events

January-February

Paris-wide sales last from January to mid-February.

February-March

Six Nations Rugby Tournament: Stade de France (see p.31). *www.rbs6nations.com*

Paris Fashion Week: The fashion event of the year. First week of March.

April

Marathon de Paris: A 42-km (26 mile) footrace through Paris, starting at the Champs-Elysées. Place de la Concorde to Château de Vincennes.

www.parismarathon.com

directory

Musée de Montmartre ❶ 1F

Quiet museum on the artistic history of Montmartre. *12 rue Cortot, T: 01 49 25 89 37, www.museedemontmartre.fr*

Musée du Montparnasse ❶ 5E

In the middle of a delightful street surrounded by artisans, the museum exhibits Montparnasse artists. *21 avenue du Maine, T: 01 42 22 91 96, www.museedumontparnasse.net*

Musée Pasteur ❷ 6C

See the rooms where the famous French chemist lived. *Institut Pasteur, 25 rue du Docteur Roux, T: 01 45 68 82 83, www.pasteur.fr*

Musée de la Poste ❷ 6D

Surprisingly interesting museum on the French postal system with more than 3,500 stamps. *34 boulevard de Vaugirard, T: 01 42 79 23 23, www.museedelaposte.fr*

Musée de la Préfecture de Police ❷ 5G

Everything concerning Parisian crime. *4 rue de la Montagne Ste-Geneviève, T: 01 44 41 52 50.*

Musée du Vin ❶ 4B

These vaults are all that remain of a wine-making monastery destroyed in the Revolution. After the tour, taste the wine. *Rue des Eaux, 5 square Charles Dickens, T: 01 45 25 63 26, www.museeduvinparis.com*

Palais de la Découverte ❷ 2C

This is the original Parisian science museum, covering every aspect of science in a user-friendly manner. It's always a hit with the kids. *Avenue Franklin D Roosevelt, T: 01 56 43 20 21, www.palais-decouverte.fr*

Pavillon de l'Arsenal ❶ 4G

This intriguing place looks at Paris's architectural make-up by presenting a mixture of plans, models and photographs. *21 boulevard Morland, T: 01 42 76 33 97, www.pavillon-arsenal.com*

Parks

Paris's parks offer areas of relative peace and tranquillity; a respite from the city hustle. For further details, go to See it, pp.2-13.

Jardin des Plants ❷ 6H

Created by Louis XIII's physicans, in the 17th-century, this royal herb garden has flourished over the centuries to become the cities principal botanical garden with over 10,000 plant species. Today it offers a peaceful retreat from the hustle of the surrounding quarter and houses the interesting **Muséum National d'Histoire Naturelle**. *36 rue Geoffroy-St-Hilaire, T: 01 40 79 56 01, www.mnhn.fr*

Palais-Royal ❷ 2F/3

This palace (closed to the public) was once the scene of wild orgies and decadence, with illicit gambling

Grand Hôtel Lévêque €€ ❷ 4C

On the classy rue Cler, this hotel may only have two stars but it puts some three-star hotels to shame. Great value for money.
29 rue Cler, T: 01 47 05 49 15, www.hotel-leveque.com

Prince Albert Wagram €€ ❶ 1D

Family-run two-star hotel close to the Arc de Triomphe (*see p.5*) and Champs-Elysées (*see p.16*). The 33 en-suite rooms are comfortably furnished with WiFi access. *28 passage Cardinet, T: 01 47 54 06 00, www.hotelprincealbert.com*

Budget

Hôtel Madeleine Opéra € ❷ 1E

This basic 25-room hotel boasts a traditional shop-style frontage in the heart of Paris's theatre and shopping districts. *12 rue Greffulhe, T: 01 47 42 26 26, www.hotel-madeleine-opera.com*

Hôtel Vivienne € ❷ 1G

Nothing complicated but a hotel that you feel at home in, offering a basic level of comfort at a very good price. *40 rue Vivienne, T: 01 42 33 13 26.*

Museums & Sights

More Paris museums. Details of main entries in See it *pp.2-13*.

Cité des Sciences et de l'Industrie Off map at ❷ 1G

Extensive science museum with many changing exhibitions and a planetarium. *La Villette, 30 avenue Coretin-Cariou, T: 01 40 05 80 00, www.cite-sciences.fr*

Musée des Arts et Métiers ❶ 3G

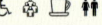

Great hands-on science museum, popular with the kids. *60 rue Réaumur, T: 01 53 01 82 00, www.arts-et-metiers.net*

Musée de l'Erotisme ❶ 1E

Museum devoted to erotic works of art. *72 boulevard de Clichy, T: 01 42 58 28 73, www.musee-erotisme.com*

Musée Grevin ❷ 1G

The French equivalent of Madame Tussaud's. *10 boulevard Montmartre, T: 01 47 70 85 05, www.grevin.com*

Musée d'Histoire de la Médecine ❷ 5G

A collection of medical instruments from ancient times to the 20th century. *Université René Descartes, 12 rue de l'Ecole-de-Médecine, T: 01 40 46 16 93.*

Musée de la Monnaie ❷ 4F

Housed in the 18th-century mint, this museum traces French currency from the Roman Empire to today. *11 quai de Conti, T: 01 40 46 55 35, www.monnaiedeparis.fr*

directory

Elysées Union €€€ ❷ 2A

A hotel with a clean, modern feel. 44 rue Hamelin, T: 01 45 53 14 95, www.elysees-union.com

Napoleon €€€ ❷ 1B

This elegant, old-world, family-run hotel features tasteful décor and the atmospheric Bivouac bar. 40 avenue de Friedland, T: 01 56 68 43 21, www.hotelnapoleonparis.com

Hôtel de Notre-Dame €€€ ❷ 5G

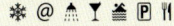

Sitting in an enviable position opposite Notre-Dame, this old-style hotel offers impeccable service. 19 rue Maître-Albert, T: 01 43 26 79 00, www.hotel-paris-notredame.com

Tronchet €€€ ❷ 1E

Tastefully decorated 34-bedroom hotel in an old mansion house in the Opéra district. 22 rue Tronchet, T: 01 47 42 26 14, www.hotel-tronchet.com

Moderate

Hôtel Caron de Beaumarchais €€ ❷ 4H

Charming hotel taking inspiration from the 18th-century mansions of the Marais, with antique furnishings and décor typical of the *art de vivre* era. 12 rue Vieille-du-Temple, T: 01 42 72 34 12, www.carondebeaumarchais.com

Hôtel du Champ-de-Mars €€ ❷ 4C

Excellent value for money in this colourful hotel. It is extremely popular so book at least a month in advance. 7 rue du Champ-de-Mars, T: 01 45 51 52 30.

Hôtel Les Jardins du Luxembourg €€ ❷ 6G

This 19th-century townhouse hotel has an intimate bohemian interior, complete with an original 1930s art deco bar counter doubling as the reception desk. The 26 rooms are small but perfectly formed for a comfortable stay in leafy surrounds. 5 Impasse Royer-Collard, T: 01 40 46 08 88, www.les-jardins-du-luxembourg.com

Saint Dominique €€ ❷ 3C

Close to the Tour Eiffel (see p.13), this hotel is full of rustic charm, with a pleasant patio for use in the summer. 62 rue St-Dominique, T: 01 47 05 51 44, www.hotelstdominique.com

Au Royal Cardinal Hôtel €€ ❷ 5H

Well-placed in the Latin Quarter, this light and airy 36 room hotel represents good value. 1 rue des Ecoles, T: 01 46 33 93 62, www.hotelroyalcardinal.com

L'Eldorado €€ ❶ 1E

Decorated in ethnic style, with plenty of charm. With doubles from €75 the value for money makes it very popular so it is advisable to book in advance. 18 rue des Dames, T: 01 45 22 35 21.

Hôtel Meurice €€€€ ❷ 2E/ ❸

❄ @ ▼ ≡ ⊨ ¶

The five-star hotel on rue de Rivoli, in the heart of Paris, boasts a glorious dining room with mosaic floor, lofty windows, gilded mirrors and ceiling frescoes, all of which recently benefited from a Philippe Starck makeover along with its new restaurant Le Dali. Pure indulgence Parisian style. *228 rue de Rivoli, T: 01 44 58 10 10, www.meuricehotel.com*

Hôtel Pergolèse €€€€ ❶ 2B

This very elegant 40-bedroom hotel, designed by Rena Dumas-Hermés, has all the touches you would expect from four-star accommodation and more. *3 rue Pergolèse, T: 01 53 64 04 04, www.hotelpergolese.com*

Hôtel Le Ritz €€€€ ❷ 2E/ ❸

❄ @ ▼ ≡ P ¶ ⊨

The choice for royalty and celebrity alike, the super-luxurious Ritz boasts 106 rooms and 56 suites, features an Ancient Greece-styled swimming pool, shopping arcade, and renowned cookery school - *Ecole Ritz Escoffier*. *15 place Vendôme, T: 01 43 16 30 30, www.ritzparis.com*

Expensive

Hôtel Amarante Beau Manoir €€€ ❷ 1E

Comfort and calm are guaranteed at this hotel, comprising 23 rooms and three suites, situated close to the upmarket shopping area of Faubourg St-Honoré. *6 rue de l'Arcade, T: 01 53 43 28 28, www.amarante-beau-manoir.com*

Hôtel Britannique €€€ ❷ 4G/ ❹

This hotel dates back to 1840, and as its name denotes, it was established by a British hotelier. Great central location for visiting the Louvre, Notre-Dame, and the Pompidou Centre. *20 avenue Victoria, T: 01 42 33 74 59, www.hotel-britannique.fr*

Hôtel Buci €€€ ❷ 4F

Near fashionable Boulevard Saint Germain, the Buci is soothingly atmospheric, with leather chairs in the lobby, potted palms and an intriguing collection of art deco paintings and statues. *22 rue de Buci, T: 01 55 42 74 74, www.bucihotel.com*

Hôtel Clos Médicis €€€ ❷ 5G

This 38-bedroom hotel has been converted from a sumptuous private mansion; the small garden and the hotel décor give a rather Provençal feel to the place. *56 rue Monsieur-le-Prince, T: 01 43 29 10 80, www.closmedicis.com*

Les Deux-Iles €€€ ❷ 5H

❄ ▲ ▼ ¶ ⊨

Situated in the heart of l'Ile St-Louis (*see p.8*), Les Deux Iles offers a very peaceful place to stay, away from the noise and bustle of the city. *59 rue St-Louis-en-l'Ile, T: 01 43 26 13 35, www.deuxiles-paris-hotel.com*

directory

For locals as well as newcomers, this Paris directory has everything you need to get the best out of the city, from what to do with the children to annual events and finding the best hotels in all categories. There are suggestions for seeking out additional museums, galleries and parks not included in earlier chapters. You'll also find listings of popular websites, entertainment magazines and local newspapers as well as a special feature on how to understand the natives.

Key to Icons

Hotels
- Room Service
- Restaurant
- Fully Licensed Bar
- En suite Bathroom
- @ Business Centre
- Health Centre
- ❄ Air Conditioning
- Ⓟ Parking

Museums
- Toilets
- Disabled Facilities
- Refreshments
- Free Admission
- Guided Tours

Places to Stay

Paris has thousands of hotel rooms, ranging from the grand and luxurious to the simple, clean and comfortable. Most very expensive hotels lie close to the Champs-Elysées. The price of a double room does not include breakfast or the *taxe de séjour*.

Luxury

Hôtel Franklin D. Roosevelt
€€€€ ❷ 2B

The Franklin Roosevelt has 48 rooms and suites all with tastefully decorated en-suites. *18 rue Clément Marot, T: 01 53 57 49 50, www.hroosevelt.com*

Price

per double room
€ budget (under €90)
€€ moderate (€90-150)
€€€ expensive (€150-300)
€€€€ deluxe (€300 +)

1 Nov: All Saints' Day, 11 Nov: Armistice 1918, 25 Dec: Christmas Day.

Telephones

Paris and its surrounding area Ile-de-France have the prefix of 01; if you are calling from outside the area, drop the 0. The international code for France is 33. To call abroud from France dial 00, then the country code e.g. 44 for the UK. To use a public telephone, buy a phone card (*Télécarte*) from *tabacs* (tobacconists), post offices and Metro stations. Some public phones use credit cards, but these can be expensive.

Emergency Numbers
Ambulance (*SAMU*): *15*
Emergency from a mobile: *112*
Fire (*Sapeurs-Pompiers*): *18*
Police: *17*

Tipping

A service charge of 10-15% is legally included in the bill. It is, however, polite to round up the bill or leave a cash tip, depending on the level of service you were given (*see p.39*).

Tours

Bus Tours

Take the weight off your feet for a couple of hours and view the Paris sights by bus.

Cityrama ❷ 3F
4 place des Pyramides,
T: 01 44 55 61 00, www.cityrama.fr

Les Cars Rouges ❷ 4A
17 quai de Grenelle,
T: 01 53 95 39 53,
www.carsrouges.com

Paris Vision ❷ 2E
214 rue de Rivoli, T: 01 42 60 30 01,
www.parisvision.com

Canal Tours

Cruise the Canal St Martin ❶ 2G-5G, built by Napoleon to connect the Marne with the Seine.

Canauxrama
13 quai de la Loire, T: 01 42 39 15 00,
www.canauxrama.com

Paris Canal
19-21 quai de la Loire,
T: 01 42 40 96 97,
www.pariscanal.com

River Tours

A sightseeing trip around the islands or a romantic dinner on the Seine.

Bateaux Parisiens ❷ 3A
Port de la Bourdonnais, T: 01 76 64 14 45,
www.bateauxparisiens.com

Boats in front of Notre-Dame along the Seine

cheques: if in doubt change them at the Banque de France, the French state bank.

Bureaux de Change

These are found at the airports, rail terminals and in shopping areas such as Avenue des Champs-Elysées (❷1B). The main ones open in office hours. Smaller agencies open longer, but check their rates carefully first. **Travelex:** *Open 8.30am-9.30pm daily. 125 avenue des Champs-Elysées, T: 01 47 20 25 14, www.travelex.com*

Credit Cards

France took to credit cards long

A French pharmacy sign

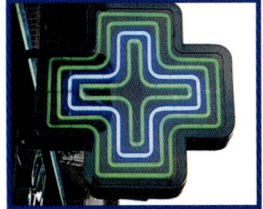

before her European neighbours: they are accepted in most shops and restaurants.
American Express:
T: 01 47 77 72 00.
Diners Club:
T: 08 10 31 41 59.
MasterCard:
T: 08 00 90 13 87.
Visa *(Carte Bleue):*
T: 08 00 90 11 79.

Night Pharmacies

The pharmacies listed below stay open after normal shopping hours.

Pharmacie Européenne de la Place de Clichy ❶ 1E
Open 24 hours. 6 place de Clichy, T: 01 48 74 65 18.

Pharmacie des Champs-Elysées ❷ 1B
Open 24 hours. 84 avenue des Champs-Elysées, T: 01 45 62 02 41.

Pharmacie Matignon ❷ 2C
Open 8.30am-2am daily. 2 rue Jean-Mermoz, T: 01 43 59 86 55.

Personal Safety

For its size, Paris is considered a safe city. However, you should take basic precautions: keep valuables concealed, stay in well-lit areas at night and look out for pickpockets in the Metro and tourist sites.

Post Offices

Main Post Office ❷ 3G
Open 7.20am-6.20am daily. 52 rue du Louvre, T: 01 40 28 76 00, www.laposte.fr

Other post offices (*La Poste*) are open 8am-7pm Mon-Fri, and 8am-12 noon Sat. Postage stamps are available from post offices, hotels, machines or the ubiquitous *tabacs* (tobacconists).

Public Holidays

1 Jan: New Year's Day, Easter Mon, 1 May: Labour Day, 8 May: Victory 1945, 20 May: Ascension Day, 30 May: Whit Monday, 14 July: Bastille Day, 15 Aug: Assumption Day,

Internet Cafés

La Baguenaude ❷ 3G/❹
Open 10am-8.4pm Mon-Sat. 30 rue Grande Truanderie, T: 01 40 26 27 74, www.labaguenaude.com

Cyber Cube ❶ 4H
Open daily 10am-10pm. 12 rue Daval, T: 01 49 29 67 67, www.cybercube.fr

Milk ❷ 3G/❹
Open 24 hours. 31 boulevard de Sébastopol, T: 08 20 00 10 00, www.milklub.com

Wi-Fi

Free Wi-Fi access is available from over 260 gardens, libraries and museums including the Pompidou Centre. Many of Paris's top hotels also have free Wi-Fi access in their public areas.

Lost Property

To claim your lost property, go to the Bureau des Objets Trouvés (❶ 6C), *36 rue des Morillons, T: 08 21 00 25 25.*

Medical Care

British nationals should carry a European Health Insurance Card (EHIC) to ensure they receive any necessary healthcare free or at a reduced cost.

SOS Médecins
Doctors with call-out service for emergencies. *T: 01 47 07 77 77.* For a list of hospitals with casualty departments, look in the phone book under Hôpital Assistance Publique or *www.aphp.fr*

SOS Dentaire
Emergency dental care. *T: 01 43 37 51 00.*

Money & Banks

Euros are divided into 100 cents and come in a variety of denominations. There are seven notes in denominations of 5, 10, 20, 50, 100, 200 and 500 euros; and eight euro coins in denominations of 1, 2, 5, 10, 20, 50 cents, 1 and 2 euros.

ATMs

Euros can be withdrawn from banks, post offices, department stores and some supermarkets. Each machine displays the logos of the cards accepted. Once you insert your card, you will be prompted to select your language. Streetside ATMs are open 24 hours.

Banks

Opening times are usually 9am-5pm Mon-Fri, or from Tues-Sat. All are closed on public holidays, often including the afternoon of the day before. Most accept travellers'

Euros notes and coins

Disabled sign

Allo Vélo ❷ 1H
Bike rentals, sales, and repairs. Accessories such as baskets, child seats, rain gear. *20 rue d'Hauteville, T: 01 40 35 36 36, www.allovelo.com*

Freescoot ❷ 5H
Vespa and Piaggio scooters for rent (includes helmet and insurance) for over-21s. Book in advance. *63 quai de la Tournelle, T: 01 44 07 06 72, www.freescoot.com*

Climate

Paris is typical of any northern European city; it can be hot in summer and cold in winter. Snow is rare but near-freezing temperatures and cold winds are frequent. Spring and autumn are normally quite temperate, while the summer months are punctuated by heavy thundery showers. Average temperatures in Jul-Aug 20°C, Dec-Jan 3°C. Average rainfall in Jul-Aug 60mm, Dec-Jan 50mm.

Disabled Access

Paris is not especially good at catering for the disabled, but with stringent EU regulations regarding accessibility, thankfully things are slowly improving.
For more details contact:
Association des Paralysés de France.
17 boulevard Auguste-Blanqui, T: 01 40 78 69 00, www.apf.asso.fr

Electricity

The French domestic electricity supply at 220V, is compatible with British 230V. All that is needed is a plug adaptor, available from larger hardware stores such as BHV (*see p.17*). The 110V appliances used in the US will need a transformer, which again is available in the larger hardware stores.

Embassies

American Embassy ❷ 2D
2 avenue Gabriel, T: 01 43 12 22 22.

Australian Embassy ❷ 4A
4 rue Jean Rey, T: 01 40 59 33 00.

British Embassy ❷ 2D
35 rue du Faubourg-St-Honoré, T: 01 44 51 31 00.

Canadian Embassy ❷ 2C
35 avenue Montaigne, T: 01 44 43 29 00.

New Zealand Embassy ❷ 1A
7 rue Léonard-de-Vinci, T: 01 45 01 43 43.

South African Embassy ❷ 3C
59 quai d'Orsay, T: 01 53 59 23 23.

form of late-night public transport is the Noctilien, which runs every 17 minutes on weekdays and every 10 minutes on weekends between 0.30am and 5.30am. Travel passes are valid, or buy a ticket from the driver for €1.50.

Taxis

Taxi ranks *(arrêt taxi)* may be found at numerous locations such as stations, and on main streets. Vacant cabs can be identified by a white sign on the roof lit up (orange means they are busy). Charges are based on time of day and area, varying between €0.86 and €1.35 per km. The minimum charge is €5.60 plus €1 per item of luggage in the boot. It is not customary to tip but it's better to round up the price.

Driving

The French drive on the right-hand side of the road but you are strongly advised not to drive in Paris. Jams build up quickly and tempers can be explosive. In addition, parking is scarce and car parks are expensive. If you bring your car, stay in a hotel with parking or find a 24-hour patrolled car park away from the centre.

Breakdown Services
Europ Assistance: *T: 01 41 85 85 85.*
Dan Dépann: *T: 08 00 25 10 00*

Car Rental

Hertz ❷ 3F
Carrousel-Louvre. *99 rue de Rivoli,*

Vélib in action

T: 01 47 03 49 12,
www.hertz.com

Europcar ❷ 3D
Terminal Air France. *Esplanade des Invalides, T: 01 44 11 03 80,*
www.europcar.fr

Avis ❷ 2E
Place de la Madeleine,
T: 01 42 66 67 58, www.avis.com

Cycle Hire

Vélib
Launched in 2007, this popular free bike scheme allows you to use one of the 20,000 bikes available from the 1000 plus bike stations *(bornes)* dotted around the city for up to 30 minutes absolutely free. You can pick-up and return the bikes to different *bornes* 24-7. They are also available for daily or weekly hire by providing your chip and pin card details in the docking machine. This is also how the €150 deposit will be taken if the bike is not returned.
T: 01 30 79 79 30,
www.velib.paris.fr

RATP Information

T: 32 46 (within France only)
T: 08 92 69 32 46 (outside France),
www.ratp.fr

Tickets & Passes

RATP **T+** tickets may be used on all Metro, RER and bus services and can be obtained from Metro stations, on buses, at tourist offices and from *tabacs* (tobacconists). Buy them individually for €1.50, or in packs of ten (*un carnet*) for €11.10.

Mobilis passes allow unlimited travel on buses, RER and Metro in various zones for one day and cost €5.60 for adults in zone 1-2 (this area covers most of the top sights).

Paris-Visite passes allow unlimited travel on buses, RER and Metro as well as the Montmartre (*see p.4*) funicular railway for 1, 2, 3 or 5 days, and divided into zones 1-3 and 1-6 (which includes travel to the airports, Versailles and Disneyland Resort Paris). In addition, it offers discounts to many top sights. A one-day pass for zones 1-3 costs €8.50. No photo required.

Carte Orange passes require a photo and are weekly (*hebdomadaire*) valid Monday to Sunday, or monthly (*mensuel*) valid from the first of the month. These are often the best value for money if you stay for a week starting Monday.

Metro

The underground system is the easiest way to navigate the city. The network runs daily from 5.20am-1.20am (2.20am on Saturdays) and is divided into five zones; 1 and 2 cover the centre.

RER

This express suburban train network interlinks with the Metro and runs from 4.45am-1.30am daily. With fewer stops, the RER is faster out to the suburbs than the metro.

Bus

Operates Monday-Saturday between 5.30am and 8.30pm with a more restricted service on some routes on Sundays. Tickets may be obtained from the driver or valid RATP passes (*see Tickets & Passes*) can be used. Tickets must be punched in the machine beside the driver on the bus, or show your pass to the driver.

Night Buses

Apart from taxis (*see right*), the only

Sign at Metro entrance

Parisian Taxi

Gare du Nord

€40 to €50 (plus €1 for each item of luggage). Depending on the time of day, the journey can take up to an hour.

From Orly

Orlybus

From the airport to Denfert-Rochereau Metro/RER station (**1** 6E) every 15 mins, taking about 40 mins. Tickets cost €6.10 and can be obtained on the bus. *T: 32 46 (within France only), www.ratp.fr*

OrlyVal

A frequent driverless-shuttle train to Antony RER operates daily from 6am-11pm and takes about 40 mins. Tickets cost €7.20. *www.orlyval.com*

Taxi

A ride into the centre costs around €35 (add €1 for each item of luggage in the boot) and the journey usually takes between 20-40 minutes.

By Rail

Six mainline rail terminals serve Paris; clockwise around the capital they are:

Gare du Nord (**1** 2G).
Gare de l'Est (**1** 2G).
Gare de Lyon (**1** 5H).
Gare d'Austerlitz (**1** 5G).
Gare Montparnasse (**2** 6D).

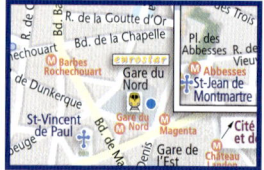

Gare St-Lazare (**2** 1E).

The **Eurostar** service runs from London St Pancras, Ebbsfleet Int'l and Ashford stations in the UK to Gare du Nord in just two hours 15 minutes from where you can connect to metro, RER and bus routes.
Eurostar (UK): *T: 01233 617575,*
Eurostar Paris: *T: 08 92 35 35 39.*

By Coach

Coaches arriving in Paris terminate at the Gare Routière Internationale Paris-Gallieni at Porte de Bagnolet, from where you can take Metro Line 3 into the centre from the Gallieni Metro station.
Eurolines: *T: 08 92 69 52 52.*

Getting Around

Paris's public transport system, RATP, covers the Metro, bus routes, suburban trains (RER) and tramways (of which there are four lines, but not near the centre).

Tourist Info

Office de Tourisme ❷ 2F
*Open 9am-7pm daily Jun-Oct; 10am to 7pm Mon-Sat, 11am-7pm Sun Nov-May. 25 rue des Pyramides,
T: 08 92 68 30 00, www.parisinfo.com*
Branches: Gare de Lyon (❶ 5H), Gare du Nord (❶ 2G), Montmartre (❶ 1G), Carrousel du Louvre (❷ 3F/❸), Anvers (❶ 1F), Paris Expo/Porte de Versailles (❶ 6B).

Arriving by Air

Paris is served by three international airports:

Roissy/Charles de Gaulle (CDG)
The largest airport serving Paris is situated 23 km (14 miles) north-east of the city. It has three terminals; the second is split into terminals A to F.
T: 01 48 62 22 80, www.adp.fr

Orly (ORY)
Situated 14 km (9 miles) south of Paris, Orly has two terminals: South (international) and West (domestic).
T: 01 49 75 15 15, www.adp.fr

Beauvais (BVA)
70 km (43 miles) north of Paris and is served by budget airlines like Ryanair. Buses run to Porte Maillot (1 hour) where you can connect to Metro line 1 into the city.
Tickets are €13. *T: 03 44 11 19 59, www.aeroportbeauvais.com*

Arriving in Paris

From Charles de Gaulle

Air France Bus
Departs every 15 to 20 minutes between 5.45am-11pm, calling at Porte Maillot and Etoile/Place Charles de Gaulle (❷ 1B). Tickets cost €14 one-way and it takes 25 mins to an hour depending on the traffic. A second route operates to Gare Montparnasse (❷ 6D) and Gare de Lyon (❷ 5H) every 30 minutes between 7am-9pm. Tickets cost €15 one-way. *T: 08 92 35 08 20 (multi-lingual schedule and fare information).*

RER
The station at Terminal 2 CDG (linked by shuttle from Terminal 1) runs the RER line B (Roissyrail) service direct to the Gare du Nord, St-Michael and Châtelet Les Halles. Trains depart every 15 mins between 4.56am-11.56pm daily and take approximately 45 mins. Tickets cost €8.20 one way. *T: 32 46 (within France only), www.ratp.fr*

Roissy Bus
Operates between airport and Opéra (❷ 1F), leaving every 15 mins from 5.45am-11pm. Travel time is about 45 mins. Tickets can be obtained on the bus, €8.60.
T: 32 46 (within France only).

Taxi
A taxi into the centre will cost from

RER sign at railway station

know it practical information

paris practical information

Although Paris has spread out to the suburbs, it is not as sprawling as most other major European cities. By far the majority of attractions are in the city centre and include more than 1,800 classified monuments, 180 museums and 145 theatres. The RATP operates a clean, modern, efficient public transport system linking all of these. The Metro, with 14 numbered lines crossing the capital, and the RER, with trains to the suburbs and main airports, are the fastest ways to get around. Buses, operating on some 60 routes, are a good way to see the city but try to avoid these during rush hours. Thanks to the recent Eurostar high-speed link from Paris Gare du Nord to London St. Pancras, the city has never been easier to reach in just two hours 15 minutes.

Exterior of Les Deux Magots

A Priori-Thé ❷ 2F/❸
These charming 19th-century tearooms make an ideal setting to meet friends and discuss life over tea and cake. *35 Galerie Vivienne, T: 01 42 97 48 75.*

Jean-Paul Hévin ❷ 2E/❸
A cosy tea room upstairs contrasts sharply with the minimalism of the shop. Sample wicked chocolate desserts and fine-leaf teas. *231 rue St-Honoré, T: 01 55 35 35 96, www.jphevin.com*

Le Café de la Mairie ❷ 5F
This café-brasserie facing St-Sulpice church is popular with both local intellectuals and young trendies, and apparently was Henry Miller's parisian café of choice. *8 place St-Sulpice, T: 01 43 26 67 82.*

Le Café Marly ❷ 3F/❸
Upmarket and giving a spectacular view of the Louvre pyramid (*see p.9*) – it's great but a little on the pricey side. *Cour Napoléon, 93 rue de Rivoli, T: 01 49 26 06 60.*

Les Deux Magots ❷ 4F
As much an institution as a café, this large and beautifully decorated venue was the favoured haunt of Rimbaud, Verlaine and Sartre. *6 place St-Germain-des-Prés, T: 01 45 48 55 25, www.lesdeuxmagots.fr*

Mariage Frères, Salon de thé et magasin ❷ 4H
A *salon de thé* where you can have a light lunch, snack or buy yourself a treat for later. Try the green-tea cake for pure indulgence or one of the many other delicious patisseries on offer. *30 rue du Bourg-Tibourg, T: 01 42 72 28 11, www.mariagefreres.com*

Afternoon tea Parisian style

taste it

A Priori-Thé in Galerie Vivienne

La Liberté Off map at ❶ 4H
Cheerful bistro in an extremely upmarket area, offering a very good selection of wines and relative value for money. *196 rue du Faubourg-St-Antoine, T: 01 43 72 11 18.*

La Palette ❷ 4F
Charming and in an area dominated by art galleries. Nibble a selection of cheeses and charcuterie and enjoy a drink: the best in the area. *43 rue de Seine, T: 01 43 26 68 15.*

Le Petit Caboulot ❶ 1E
A really good, old-fashioned bistro with a predictable menu (duck, foie gras, goat's cheese and tarte tatin) done exceptionally well. *6 place Jacques-Froment, T: 01 46 27 19 00.*

Le Réservoir Off map at ❶ 5H
Popular with Paris's showbiz fraternity, this converted textile warehouse offers a chance to let your hair down with live music nightly after 11pm. *16 rue de la Forge-Royale, T: 01 43 56 39 60.*

Le Sélect ❶ 5E
Old brasserie that became an artists' meeting place during the 1920s and 30s for the likes of Matisse, F. Scott Fitzgerald and Picasso. Fortunately the area still retains a little of its old artistic atmosphere. *99 boulevard du Montparnasse, T: 01 45 48 38 24.*

La Tartine ❷ 4H
Paris's oldest wine bar, a few blocks east of Hôtel de Ville, is friendly and inexpensive, with a surprisingly good menu – as well as the namesake tartines (sandwiches). Decor is classic art deco, and the clientele mainly young locals. *24 rue de Rivoli. T: 01 42 72 76 85.*

Le Viaduc Café ❶ 5H
Situated under a lovely arch among the galleries of Avenue Daumesnil, this is the perfect bar to stay up late in; it's open until 2am daily. *43 avenue Daumesnil, T: 01 44 74 70 70, www.viaduc-cafe.fr*

Cafés

Angélina ❷ 2E/ ❸
It is not unknown to queue to gain access to this famed salon de thé but it is well worth a visit to savour their renowned hot chocolate. *226 rue de Rivoli, T: 01 42 60 82 00.*

L'Appartement Café ❶ 3G
Situated in a little road next to the Musée Picasso (see p.10) gardens. Relax over a fortifying cocktail or coffee and a lingering game of chess. *18 rue des Coutures-St-Gervais, T: 01 48 87 12 22.*

Le Café Thoumieux ❷ 3C
Very pleasant tapas bar; seat yourself on one of the long wooden benches and enjoy a cocktail along with good, hearty little tapas dishes, which are available after 7pm. *79 rue Saint Dominique, T: 01 47 05 49 75, www.thoumieux.com*

Breakfast in Paris
For years the traditional French breakfast consisted of half a buttered baguette and a large bowl of café au lait in which to dunk it. Today this has been taken over by what we term the 'continental' breakfast – black coffee and a croissant or a pain au chocolat – a flaky pastry filled with delicious dark chocolate.

Les Couleurs ❶ 3H
Kitschy; frequented by young artists and would-be intellectuals, with dance music on Friday, Saturday and Sunday nights. *117 rue St-Maur, T: 01 43 57 95 61, www.cafe-lescouleurs.com*

Le Cox ❶ 4G
Small bar in the Marais, popular with the local gay community and often packed to the gills. At quieter times, you may get a seat on the little terrace overlooking the street. *15 rue des Archives, T: 01 42 72 08 00, www.coxbar.fr*

La Divette de Montmartre ❶ 1G
There is a lively mix of clientele in this bar decorated with hundreds of record sleeves (oldies should remember these!). *36 rue Marcadet, T: 01 46 06 19 64.*

L'Entrepôt ❶ 6D
A warehouse now converted to house a bar, restaurant and arts cinema. *7–9 rue Francis-de-Pressensé, T: 01 45 40 07 50, www.lentrepot.fr*

Grand verre de vin rouge

La Fourmi ❶ 2F
Popular with the locals, this surprisingly friendly café bar will certainly leave you wanting to come back again. *74 rue des Martyrs, T: 01 42 64 70 35.*

Kong ❷ 3G/❹
This bar-restaurant with its Philippe Starck-designed interior serves beautiful food for beautiful people including a certain Carrie Bradshaw from *Sex and the City*. Expect to pay handsomely for the whole manga kitsch experience. *1 rue du Pont Neuf, T: 01 40 39 09 00, www.kong.fr*

between your Left Bank shopping. Serving an eclectic menu from local, fresh produce, you can't go wrong with any of these reasonably priced dishes. *11 rue Dupin, T: 01 42 22 64 56, www.epidupin.com*

Gaya €€€€ ❷ 4E

With Michelin star chef Pierre Gagnaire at the helm, this fish restaurant offers cutting-edge gastro-cuisine incorporating the current trend for molecular cooking, which groups unlikely ingredients together for a taste sensation. *44 rue du Bac, T: 01 45 44 73 73, www.pierre-gagnaire.com*

Bars & Brasseries

À la Cloche des Halles ❷ 3G/❹

Named after the bell hanging above the bar that was used to sound the end of trading at the old Les Halles markets, this very small wine bar has an impressive range of wines and locally sourced cheese and sausage. *28 rue Coquillière, T: 01 42 36 93 89.*

Le Bar du Marché ❷ 4F

This is a popular student bar on the very lively Rue de Buci. The bar and the pavement – which acts as the terrace in summer – are never empty. *75 rue de Seine, T: 01 43 26 55 15.*

La Belle Hortense ❷ 4H

Great bar for wine buffs and literary enthusiasts: you can buy wine from the extensive choice on display, choose a book and relax in this bar-cum-library-cum-wine store. Every Wednesday there are book readings. *31 rue Vieille-du-Temple, T: 01 48 04 71 60.*

Brasserie Lipp ❷ 4E

Indulge in delicious Alsace dishes, beers and wines in this renowned Belle Epoque fantasia. *151 boulevard Saint Germain, T: 01 45 48 53 91, www.brasserie-lipp.fr*

Buddha Bar ❷ 2D

The taste of the décor is quixotic but it is well worth the visit to see the very conspicuous giant figure of Buddha. A popular haunt with the stars, but expect to pay over the top for average food. *8 rue Boissy-d'Anglas, T: 01 53 05 90 00, www.buddha-bar.com*

Le Café Charbon ❶ 3H

Lovely old-fashioned bar retaining a fin de siècle atmosphere. Brasserie food (steak, sausages) is available in the evenings and also during the day at the weekend. *109 rue Oberkampf, T: 01 43 57 55 13.*

Back street brasserie

are well worth the queues and busy atmosphere. *47 rue de Bretagne, T: 01 42 72 36 26.*

Mansouria €€-€€€ ❶ 4H

One of the best Moroccan restaurants in Paris, excellent food, discreet waiters, soft lighting: a place that you will willingly revisit. *11 rue Faidherbe, T: 01 43 71 00 16.*

404 €-€€ ❷ 4H

Expect an entertaining evening at this Kasbah-styled setting, where you can indulge in spicy tangines and mint cocktails amongst Moroccan lamps and lively waiters. *9 Rue des Graviliers, T: 01 42 74 57 81.*

À la carte menu

Spanish

Fogon St-Julien €€ ❷ 5G

Situated close to the charming St-Julien-le-Pauve church, this tiny place is the perfect venue to enjoy delicious tapas and a range of other Iberian specialities. *10 rue St-Julien-le-Pauvre, T: 01 43 54 31 33.*

Vegetarian

Au Grain de Folie €-€€ ❶ 1G

Tiny restaurant serving a good mix of vegetarian and vegan dishes that will not strain your purse strings. *24 rue de la Vieuville, T: 01 42 58 15 57.*

La Victoire Suprême du Cœur € ❷ 4H

You can still expect the fabulous mushroom terrine and seitan (wheat gluten) "steak" in this long established restaurant following its move from Les Halles to Le Marais. *7-31 rue du Bourg Tibourg, T: 01 40 41 95 03, www.vscoeur.com*

Tips on Tipping
Restaurants in Paris have to display their menus and prices where customers can see them. These prices include service, but a tip is always appreciated. It can range from a few euros to five per cent of the total bill.

Bistros

Le Timbre €-€€ ❷ 6E

English chef Chris Wright runs, as the name suggests, a postage stamp-sized bistro more French in style and menu that many French-run bistros. Popular with the locals thanks to classics like *parmentier de queue de boeuf* (oxtail and mash). *3 rue Sainte Beuve, T: 01 45 49 10 40, www.restaurantletimbre.com*

L'Epi Dupin €-€€ ❷ 5E

This rustic dining room close by Le Bon Marché makes a perfect stop off

Ma Bourgogne €€€ ❶ 4G
Situated underneath the arcades that surround the beautiful Place des Vosges, this restaurant offers simple but tasty French regional cuisine. *19 place des Vosges, T: 01 42 78 44 64.*

Le Procope €€€€ ❷ 4F
The oldest café in Paris (1686), now a comfortable brasserie, serves traditional French food in an interior redolent with French political and

Place des Vosges outside Ma Bourgogne

literary history. Worth it for the atmosphere as much as for the cuisine traditionnelle. *13 rue de l'Ancienne-Comédie, T: 01 40 46 79 00, www.procope.com*

Senderens €€€€ ❷ 2E/❸
A real gastronomic delight; the two Michelin stars are well-earned by chef Alain Senderens in this simplied version of his previous Lucas Carlton restaurant. This is definitely the place to come for a special occasion. *9 place de la Madeleine, T: 01 42 65 22 90, www.senderens.fr*

Italian

Le Bistrot Napolitain € ❷ 1C
This small bistro, close by the Champs-Elysées, offers no fuss authentic stone-baked pizzas and fresh pasta within a lively setting. The low prices and large portions will also make you smile. *18 avenue Franklin Roosevelt, T: 01 45 62 08 37.*

Findi €€ ❷ 2B
An elegant restaurant where you can

La Vinoteca transportation

get a real taste of Italy. *24 avenue George V, T: 01 47 20 14 78, www.findi.net*

La Vinoteca €€-€€€ ❷ 1C
Relatively new on the block, this superb Italian enjoys an extensive regional wine list and gourmet dishes within a sleek interior. *32 rue de Courcelles, T: 01 53 96 07 68.*

North African

Chez Omar € ❶ 3G
This permanently busy North African restaurant is famous for its delightful cous cous and *merquez* dishes that

The ultra-modern interior of Tokyo Eat

two specialities are choucroute and seafood. *5-7 rue de la Bastille, T: 01 42 72 87 82, www.bofingerparis.com*

Chez Chartier € ❷ 1F

This vast restaurant, established in 1896, serves more than 1,500 meals a day. The food is pretty average but the beaux-arts décor makes a visit worthwhile. Reservations only for large groups. *7 rue du Faubourg Montmartre, T: 01 47 70 86 29.*

Claude Sainlouis €€€ ❷ 4E

Attracting the well-heeled sophisticates of St-Germain and known locally as the 'president's restaurant' after the many political portraits hanging from the walls. It is also known for its top-quality meat dishes. *27 rue du Dragon, T: 01 45 48 29 68, http://claudestlouis.com*

Le Dôme du Marais €€€ ❶ 4G

An ideal place for a romantic dinner for two, especially in the summer when you can sit outside on the pretty terrace. *53 bis, rue des Francs-Bourgeois, T: 01 42 74 54 17.*

La Fermette Marbeuf €€€€ ❷ 2C

A superb listed dining area in a fine example of Belle-Epoque décor. A magical place that should be visited at least once. *5 rue Marbeuf, T: 01 53 23 08 00, www.fermettemarbeuf.com*

Le Georges €€€€ ❷ 3H/❹

Situated atop the Pompidou Centre (*see p.6*), this restaurant boasts great views of the city. Reasonable food served in a large dining area made of rubber and aluminium. *Centre Georges-Pompidou, T: 01 44 78 47 99, www.centrepompidou.fr*

Le Jules Verne €€€€ ❶ 4C/❷ 4A

Forget meeting at the Empire State, when in *gai Paris* the ultimate dinner date has to be in the recently re-furbished Jules Verne restaurant on the second floor of the Eiffel Tower. Romance and delightful food in spades. Reservations essential. *Eiffel Tower, Champ-de-Mars, T: 01 45 55 61 44, www.lejulesverne-paris.com*

Entrance to La Fermette Marbeuf

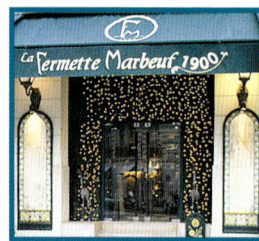

Price Guide
Prices are for a three-course meal for one without alcohol.
€ = under 30 euros
€€ = between 30-40 euros
€€€ = between 40-50 euros
€€€€ = above 50 euros

Asian

Au Coin des Gourmets € ❷ 5G
Always packed and offering specialities that one rarely finds in other Asian restaurants in Paris: a fusion between eastern and western-style cooking. *5 rue Dante, T: 01 43 26 12 92.*

Chez Vong €€ ❷ 3H/❹
Centrally located near the Pompidou Centre, this stylish restaurant has a refined decor, a wide choice of excellent Chinese dishes and good service. *10 rue de la Grande-Truanderie, T: 01 40 26 09 36, www.chez-vong.com*

Tokyo Eat €€ ❷ 3B
Located in the super-hip Palais de Tokyo, this is a stylishly modern yet inexpensive restaurant offering Asian fusion dishes accompanied by DJs. *13 avenue du Président Wilson, T: 01 47 20 00 29, www.palaisdetokyo.com*

Belgian

Bouillon Racine €€€ ❷ 5G
Magnificent art nouveau restaurant in the Latin Quarter; sample the excellent cuisine accompanied by one of a great selection of beers. *3 rue Racine, T: 01 44 32 15 60, www.bouillon-racine.com*

Soft lighting for dining in Claude Sainlouis

Eastern European

La Crypte de Polska € ❷ 2E/❸
This unique atmospheric restaurant in the basement of the church of Our Lady of the Assumption offers solid, tasty Polish fare with lots of pork and cabbage dishes served among 17th-century vaults. *1 place Maurice Barrès T: 01 42 60 43 33.*

French

Bofinger €€ ❶ 4H
A famous brasserie popular with tourists and performers coming from the Opera Bastille close by. The

taste it places to eat and drink

paris places to eat and drink

This pleasure-loving city has gourmet cuisine with grand, Michelin-starred establishments as well as numerous small restaurants serving traditional regional dishes. Seasonal specialities, from summer salads and fruit dishes to the cool-weather oysters served fresh outside brasseries and the cheese dishes of winter are all part of the food experience. In richly decorated dining rooms or intimate bistros, dining is an event as much as a mere meal. Paris is also a cosmopolitan city, with many influences from its former colonies in Asia and North and West Africa. Many other nations have also brought their culinary contributions. So dining, whether in a sumptuous restaurant or intimate bistro, creperie or pizzeria, is part of the fun in this exciting city.

View along the River Seine showing beautiful tree-lined boulevards

T: 01 42 74 22 77,
www.theatredelaville-paris.com

Théâtre des Champs-Elysées ❷ 2B
Concerts from classic to modern, opera to dance, plus recitals of chamber music. *15 avenue Montaigne, T: 01 49 52 50 50, www.theatrechampselysees.fr*

Sport

Cycling
Go into a Parisian bar during the month of July and the TV screen will show a pack of cyclists peddling up a winding mountain pass. This is accompanied by heated debate over the famed yellow jersey – the trophy for the leading cyclist of the day. The Tour de France covers 4,000 km (2,486 miles) in three weeks, ending in a mad sprint down the Champs-Elysées. *www.letour.fr*

Horse Racing
The Parisians are crazy about horse racing and the betting that goes with it. Many bars advertise PMU, the nationalised betting shop. The most prestigious flat race (one of the richest in the world) is the *Grand Prix de l'Arc de Triomphe*, run in October at Longchamp, Bois de Boulogne. *www.france-galop.com*

Rugby & Football
Parc des Princes (Off map at ❶ 6A) is home to Paris St-Germain (football) and Le Racing (rugby). *24 rue du Commandant-Guilaud, T: 01 47 43 71 71, www.leparcdesprinces.fr*
The **Stade de France** hosts all the international rugby matches such as the Six Nations tournament. *Rue de Pressensé, T: 01 55 93 00 00, www.stadefrance.com*

Tennis
The French Open is held during the the last week of May/first week of June at Roland-Garros (❶ 5A). Ticket reservation begins at least six months before the tournament begins. See website for further details. *2 avenue Gordon Bennett, T: 01 47 43 48 00, www.rolandgarros.fr*

The popular Tour de France races down the Champs-Elysées

Opéra de Paris Garnier in full floodlit glory

Theatre & Classical Music

For information concerning theatres, contact Centre National du Théâtre, *134 rue Legendre, T: 01 44 61 84 85, www.cnt.asso.fr*

Comédie Française, Salle Richelieu ❷ 3F/❸
Founded in 1680, this is one of the stalwarts of Parisian theatre. The Salle Richelieu offers classical productions such as Molière and contemporary pieces. *2 rue de Richelieu, T: 01 44 58 15 15, www.comedie-francaise.fr*

Odéon Théâtre de l'Europe ❷ 5F
France's most historic theatre has been a centre for pan-European artistic collaboration. *Place de l'Odéon, T: 01 44 85 40 40, www.theatre-odeon.fr*

La Salle Pleyel ❶ 2C
Following a mammoth two-year renovation project, this is the capital's best classical music venue. *252 rue du Faubourg-St-Honoré, T: 01 42 56 13 13, www.sallepleyel.fr*

Théâtre National de Chaillot ❷ 3A
Contemporary works, ballet and musical drama as well as regular evenings with poets and artists. *1 place du Trocadéro, T: 01 53 65 30 00, www.theatre-chaillot.fr*

Théâtre de la Ville ❷ 4G/❹
This is the city's very best venue for contemporary theatre and dance as well as world music concerts. Twinned with the Théâtre les Abbesses (*31 rue des Abbesses,* ❶ 1E) to provide great coverage of modern works. *2 place du Châtelet,*

Welcome to the cheap seats...

If you are prepared to brave the long queues and are not too fussy on which play you see then the same day-half price ticket kiosks located at the Place de la Madeleine and the Esplanade de la Gare du Montparnasse are a good option. *Open Tues-Sat 12.30pm-7.45pm, Sun 12.30pm-3.45pm.*

venue. *2 bis, rue des Taillandiers,
T: 01 48 06 50 70, www.la-scene.com*

Jazz

Le Baiser Salé ❶ 3G/❹
Intimate venue playing blues, jazz and electric jazz from 10pm.
*58 rue des Lombards,
T: 01 42 33 37 71,
www.lebaisersale.com*

Le Caveau de la Huchette ❷ 4G
Expect quality big band and be-bop in this Left Bank cellar, which has been swinging for more than 60 years. *5 rue de la Huchette,
T: 01 43 26 65 05,
www.caveaudelahuchette.fr*

Le Duc des Lombards ❶ 3G/❹
Decked out in wood and red velvet, this club attracts bands from all over the world, playing jazz, blues and fusion. *42 rue des Lombards,
T: 01 42 33 22 88,
www.ducdeslombards.com*

Le New Morning ❷ 1H
A club that always stays in fashion attracting big names and local bands playing cutting-edge jazz, blues and pop. *7-9 rue des Petites Ecuries,
T: 01 45 23 51 41,
www.newmorning.com*

Le Sunset/Le Sunside ❶ 3G/❹
Going strong since 1983, this interesting split venue runs traditional jazz at Sunside and electric and fusion jazz downstairs at Sunset. *60 rue des Lombards,
T: 01 40 26 46 60,
www.sunset-sunside.com*

Opera

Opéra Bastille ❶ 4H
Architect Carlos Ott's radical design was opened by François Mitterrand as part of the celebrations of the bicentenary of the Revolution in 1989. The 2,700 seat venue is home to the Opéra National de Paris. Its striking façade is currently undergoing renovation work until 2009 but pedestrian access remains unaffected. *120 rue de Lyon,
T: 01 72 29 35 35,
www.opera-de-paris.fr*

Palais Garnier ❷ 1F
Designed by its namesake, Charles Garnier, in 1862 this opera house epitomises the affluence of the city under the Second Empire. The interior is very grand, with a marble staircase and domed foyer. The auditorium seats more than 2,000, who peer over a vast stage. Most opera is performed at the Bastille (*see above*) but ballet is still produced here. *Place de l'Opéra,
T: 01 72 29 35 35, www.opera-de-paris.fr*

Radical façade of the Opéra Bastille

The spherical dome of La Géode

Le Latina ❷ 3H/❹
Lying in a lovely area of the Marais, the Latina specialises in recent and classic films from all over Europe.
20 rue du Temple, T: 01 42 78 47 86, www.lelatina.com

Clubs

Les Bains Douches ❷ 3H
Catch a glimpse of the up-and-coming stars who come here in droves to pose. Dress neatly or you won't make it past the overly fastidious doorman. *7 rue du Bourg-l'Abbé, T: 01 48 87 01 80, www.lesbainsdouches.net*

Le Gibus ❶ 3G
This basement venue attracts some big name DJs. An eclectic mix of RnB, hip hop, house and techno; not bad for a one time punk hangout.
18 rue du Faubourg-du-Temple, T: 01 47 00 78 88, www.gibus.fr

La Java ❶ 2H
Known as the venue where Edith Piaf made her deput, La Java now plays host to salsa, merengue and zouk as well as top DJs providing the very best of Latino tunes.
105 rue du Faubourg-du-Temple, T: 01 42 02 20 52, www.la-java.fr

Queen ❷ 1B
Theoretically this is a gay club but in fact it is one of the capital's most popular and buzzing clubs right across the board. Plays mainly house music. *102 avenue des Champs-Elysées, T: 01 53 89 08 90, www.queen.fr*

Le Rex Club ❷ 1G
This club sealed its reputation in the 1980s for playing house and techno, and it is still going strong. Some of the world's most famous DJs visit to liven things up. *5 boulevard Poissonnière, T: 01 42 36 10 96, www.rexclub.com*

La Scène Bastille ❶ 4H
A venue reminiscent of a New York club, also doubles as a concert

Show stopping production at Crazy Horse

Folies Bergère ❶ 2F
Paris's oldest music hall still struts its stuff with the best. The girls in their exotic costumes attract customers in their thousands. *32 rue de Richer, T: 0892 68 16 50, www.foliesbergere.com*

Le Lido ❷ 1B
Scantily dressed dancers, lasers and inventive choreography go to make a dazzling spectacle of a show. *116 bis avenue des Champs-Elysées, T: 01 40 76 56 10, www.lido.fr*

Moulin Rouge ❶ 1E
The home of the can-can is a must for every cabaret-loving tourist. *82 boulevard de Clichy, T: 01 53 09 82 82, www.moulinrouge.com*

Cinemas

Le Champo ❷ 5G
Situated in the heart of the Latin Quarter, this cinema screens classic old movies, both French and international. *51 rue des Ecoles, T: 01 43 54 51 60, www.lechampo.com*

La Géode ❶ 1G
An astounding architectural feat made from a 36-m (118-ft) diameter steel sphere reflecting the buildings around it. Giant screen, reclining seats and surround-sound make for a state-of-the-art experience. *Cité des Sciences et de l'Industrie (see p.57), 26 avenue Corentin-Cariou, T: 01 39 17 10 00, www.lageode.fr*

Grand Action ❷ 5H
On the Left Bank; a good place to revisit all those old Hollywood classics and sink into nostalgia. *5 rue des Ecoles, T: 01 43 54 47 62, www.legrandaction.com*

Le Grand Rex ❷ 1G
Housed in a listed art deco building, this cinema has one of the largest auditoriums in Paris. This is a great place to see blockbuster action movies. Le Grand Rex also doubles as a concert venue. *1 boulevard Poissonnière, T: 08 92 68 05 96, www.legrandrex.com*

Façade of the Folies Bergère

watch it

What's On

To find out what's on, get **L'Officiel des Spectacles** or **Pariscope** published on Wednesdays and available at all newsstands (Presse). The monthly **Where** magazine is available at all tourist locations and in some hotels and restaurants. The Paris Convention and Visitors Bureau (see p.46) has information available on venues, times and tickets: *25 rue des Pyramides, www.parisinfo.com*

Tickets

Buy tickets from the venue or at:

Fnac ❷ 3G/❹
*Open 10am-7.30pm Mon-Sat.
Forum les Halles (see p.20),
T: 0825 020 020,
www.fnac.com*

Virgin Megastore ❷ 2C
*Open 10am-midnight Mon-Sat,
12-midnight Sun. 52-60 avenue des Champs-Elysées (see p.20),
T: 01 49 53 50 00.*

Cabaret

L'Ane Rouge ❶ 2C
Dine and be entertained by a troupe of satirical young comics. *3 rue Laugier, T: 01 47 64 45 77, www.anerougeparis.com*

Au Lapin Agile ❶ 1H inset
Traditional songs and cabaret. Very popular with tourists. *22 rue des Saules, T: 01 46 06 85 87, www.au-lapin-agile.com*

Crazy Horse Saloon ❷ 2B
Following a revamp at the end of 2007, Crazy Horse now performs some of the most risqué cabarets with dazzling high-tech panache. *12 ave George V, T: 01 47 23 32 32, www.lecrazyhorseparis.com*

Don Camilo ❷ 4E
A St-Germain institution. This veteran cabaret offers dining and entertainment at reasonable prices. *10 rue des Sts-Pères, T: 01 42 60 82 84.*

The world's most famous nightclub still pulls in the crowds

watch it entertainment

paris entertainment

The only problem you may have choosing entertainment in Paris is its sheer range, from the lavish opera houses and grand theatres serving up extravagant and colourful spectacles, to local theatres performing all manner of contemporary pieces. Why not catch a live music concert, a flamboyant cabaret show or have a night on the tiles at an über trendy nightclub? Cinema-lovers can watch the latest French and European-language films, old classics or obscure oddities from the archives. Or if sport is more your thing Paris will not disappoint, with football and rugby at the Parc des Princes, tennis at Roland-Garros, or horse racing and cycling in the Bois du Boulogne. Failing that, there is always a game of boules happening in the city gardens, which the locals may let you join in with if you are *très gentil*.

Poilâne ❷ 5E, 5B
Since 1936, the demand for the famous *pain Poilâne* – a leavened bread baked in a wood-fired oven – has continued to grow, as can be seen by the daily queue outside the shop. Take-away sandwiches are also available. *8 rue du Cherche-Midi, T: 01 45 48 42 59.*
Branch: *49 boulevard de Grenelle, T: 01 45 79 11 49, www.poilane.fr*

Sportswear

Au Vieux Campeur ❷ 5G
Part of a chain of shops, 16 of which are around the Sorbonne (*see p.4*),

Delicious fromage from Fauchon

with several in the Rue des Ecoles. Each shop has its own speciality (skiing, skating or hiking). They are reputed for the quality of their outdoor goods and high level of service. **Branch:** *48 rue des Ecoles, T: 01 53 10 48 48, www.au-vieux-campeur.fr*

Décathlon ❷ 2E/❸ & ❶ 2C
A huge choice of quality sportswear and equipment at reasonable prices. Expect everything from cycling gear and rackets to water skiing and fishing equipment. Hire service available. *23 boulevard de la Madeleine, T: 01 55 35 97 55.*
Branch: *26 avenue de Wagram, T: 01 45 72 66 88, www.decathlon.fr*

Toys

Apache ❷ 3G/❹ & ❶ 4H
Expect to find everything to keep the kids amused, including a staffed play area, while you sneak off for a well deserved drink at the conveniently placed bar. **Branches:** *Forum Les Halles, T: 01 44 88 52 00; 84 rue du Faubourg St-Antoine,*

T: 01 53 46 60 10, www.apache.fr

Au Nain Bleu ❶ 2D
The city's most famous toy store (originally sited on the Rue St-Honoré from 1836), it houses an impressive array of quality toys over three floors. A wonderful retreat for both children and adults. *5 boulevard Malesherbes, T: 01 42 65 20 00, www.aunainbleu.com*

Taxing Issues
The standard rate of value-added tax (*TVA*) in France is 19.6 per cent, although certain goods can range from five per cent to 25 per cent. Non-EU citizens who have been in France for less than three months can, in certain cases, reclaim some of the VAT on purchases. There are, many restrictions attached to this. The large stores keep the relevant forms (*bordereau de détaxe*) and will be able to explain the procedures.

all tastefully displayed in this eclectic mix of homewares. *29 rue St-Sulpice, T: 01 40 46 97 47.*

Food & Wine

Androüet ❷ 6G
More than 200 varieties of gourmet artisans' cheese to choose from, all of which are matured on the premises in curing cellars.
Branches: *134 rue Mouffetard, T: 01 45 87 85 05; 37 rue de Verneuil, T: 01 42 61 97 55; 93 rue de Cambronne, T: 01 47 83 32 05; www.androuet.com*

Fauchon ❷ 2E/❸
The elaborate window displays are a clear indication that this is one of Paris's best food shops and chocolatiers. *26 place de la Madeleine, T: 01 70 39 38 00, www.fauchon.com*

Hédiard ❷ 2E/❸
Established in 1854, this expert grocer sells fine preserves, delicatessen and spices with exemplary customer service. You will be treated like a queen as you select your produce but expect to pay a premium for this royal treatment. There is also a fine restaurant upstairs

Traditional haven of Legrand Filles et Fils

should you need a shopping pit-stop. *21 place de la Madeleine, T: 01 43 12 88 88, www.hediard.fr*

Legrand Filles et Fils ❷ 2F/❸
This charming old shop attracts tourists and local connoisseurs with its biscuits, sweets and fine wines. *1 rue de la Banque and Galerie Vivienne, T: 01 42 60 07 12, www.caves-legrand.com*

Luscious window display at Fauchon

Glittering window dressing at Hermès

travel guides on two floors. *248 rue de Rivoli, T: 01 44 77 88 99, www.whsmith.fr*

Clothing & Accessories

There are designer boutiques and stores clustered all around the Champs-Elysées and Rue du Faubourg-St-Honoré (see p.16 & 17).

Hermès ❷ 2D

Amble with pleasure through the bags, silk scarves and jewellery. Although the prices are incredibly high, you may find something to suit your budget. *24 rue du Faubourg-St-Honoré, T: 01 40 17 47 17, www.hermes.com*

Versace ❷ 2B

This chic store carries expensive women's clothing as well as accessories and handbags on several levels. Exotic evening wear and household accessories of the vulgarly expensive kind. *41 rue Francois 1er, T: 01 47 42 88 02, www.versace.com*

Yves Saint-Laurent ❷ 5F

Known for precise tailoring and stupendous pricing, Paris boasts two boutiques around the St-Suplice: one dedicated to men and one to women. Expect a wide choice of exquisite clothing, accessories and shoes. Women's shop: *6 place St-Sulpice, T: 01 43 29 43 00*. Men's shop: *12 place St-Sulpice, T: 01 43 26 84 40, www.ysl.com*

Furniture & Design

Colette ❷ 2E/❸

Paris's ultra-trendy shop for luxury goods from top designers – clothing, gadgets, jewellery – and a designer water bar downstairs. *213 rue Saint-Honore, T: 01 55 35 33 90, www.colette.fr*

Maison de Famille ❷ 5F

Soft furnishings, cutlery and furniture

Colourful threads on display at Colette

buy it

buy it

> **Sale Time**
> The word for sale in French is *solde*. Sales normally occur twice a year; at the beginning of January, when they last for a few weeks, and in July, when bargains include summer clothes as the shops restock for the winter season.

medieval in atmosphere. *Open 9am-1pm Tue-Sun. Rue Mouffetard to Place de la Contrescarpe.*

Antiques

Louvre des Antiquaires ❷ 3F/❹
As the largest covered antiques centre in France, you'll be spoilt for choice amongst the 250 plus antique dealers spread over three floors. To help narrow down your search the aisles are separated into themes such as jewellery, paintings and weapons. *Open 11am-7pm Tue-Sun. 2 place du Palais-Royal, T: 01 42 97 27 27, www.louvre-antiquaires.com*

Books & Music

See also Shakespeare & Company, *p.16*.

Fnac ❶ 4H & ❷ 3G/❹
This establishment, with stores in the Bastille, Les Halles and throughout France, is devoted to books, music, electronic goods and photographic equipment and concert tickets (*see p.26*). *4 place de la Bastille, T: 0825 020 020.* **Branch:** *1-7 rue Pierre Lescot, Forum les Halles, www.fnac.com*

Galignani ❷ 2E/❸
This charming wood-panelled bookshop was the first in France to feature a section dedicated entirely to English books. *224 rue de Rivoli, T: 01 42 60 76 07.*

Gibert Joseph ❷ 5G
A huge variety of new and second-hand books are on offer on five floors. The basement has a good range of travel books as well as works in English. *26-34 boulevard St-Michel, T: 01 44 41 88 88, www.gibertjoseph.com*

Virgin Megastore ❶ 2G/❷ 2C
The Virgin Megastore offers an incomparable choice of musical styles on CD, as well as videos, DVDs, computer games and concert tickets (*see p.26*). It is not the cheapest place in town but the sheer size makes it worth a visit. *52-60 avenue des Champs-Elysées, T: 01 49 53 50 00,* **Branch:** *Place du 11-Nov-1918, T: 01 44 65 95 41, www.virginmegastore.fr*

WHSmith ❷ 2E/❸
A large, well-stocked English-language bookshop with an excellent collection of books, periodicals and

> **Survival Guide**
> Parisian shop assistants are all aspiring models who dress to kill. They will also ignore you. Don't be intimidated; walk up to them, smile and say '*Bonjour*'. Once on your side, they are helpful and professional – if sometimes a bit too honest.

Marché d'Aligre ❶ 5H

This bustling market is one of the most colourful in the capital, with a North African feel. The 19th-century covered market is where you can find some of the best cheese and charcuterie, and all at the lowest prices. *Open 8am-1pm Tue-Sun. Place d'Aligre.*

Marché Richard Lenoir ❶ 4H

Starting at the Place de la Bastille and stretching northwards along the tree-lined Boulevard Richard Lenoir, this sizeable open-air market provides a dizzying range of meats, fish and vegetables. It is at its most lively on Sundays. *Open 9am-1pm Thur & Sun. Boulevard Richard Lenoir.*

Marché Raspail ❷ 5E

Although the produce at this rather snooty organic market comes to you straight from the farmer, the prices are astronomical. At least you will know the provenance of everything you buy and quality is guaranteed. *Open Tue, Fri & Sun am. Boulevard Raspail between Rue du Cherche-Midi and Rue de Rennes.*

Other organic markets include Marché Batignolles (❶ 2E) *open Sat 9am-1pm. Boulevard des Batignolles.*

Marché aux Fleurs et aux Oiseaux ❷ 4G/❹

Superbly positioned on the Ile-de-la-Cité (*see p.7*) next to the Palais de Justice. From Monday to Saturday, the market sells a large variety of flowers, but on Sunday it's transformed into a bird market. *Open 8am-7pm daily. Place Louis-Lépine.*

Marché Rue Mouffetard ❷ 6H

This is one of the oldest markets in Paris. It has become touristy and is often over-priced but is still known for its fruit, vegetables and charcuterie. The architecture and adjacent lanes are positively

Colourful produce in Marché Rue Mouffetard

buy it

doubt the most chic, offering a large range of clothing for men (ground floor) and women (first floor). It is also noted for its exquisite food hall. *24 rue de Sèvres, T: 01 44 39 80 00, www.lebonmarche.fr*

Galeries Lafayette ❷ 1E, 6E
With a vast glass dome, this store – dating from the Belle-Epoque – is dedicated to food and fashion, with an excellent designer concession on the first floor. *40 boulevard Haussmann, T: 01 42 82 34 56, www.galerieslafayette.com.* **Branch:** *22 rue du Départ, T: 01 45 38 52 87*

Monoprix ❷ 2C
This chain, with nearly 50 locations all over Paris, has quality goods at reasonable prices. Stores usually have a grocery section on one floor and clothing, home and beauty sections on others, besides a wide choice of clothing for men, women and children, kitchenware and toiletries. It also offers delivery service, photo booths and photocopying at most

The foodhall of Galeries Lafayette

branches. *52 avenue des Champs-Elysées, T: 01 53 77 65 65, www.monoprix.fr*

TATI ❶ 1F
This store has the reputation of having the lowest prices in Paris, which could go some way to explain the crowds through which one has to battle. Although there is nothing exceptional here, it is worth keeping your eyes open for the occasional bargain. *4 boulevard Rochechouart, T: 01 55 29 52 20, www.tati.fr*

Markets

Bouquinistes ❷ 4G, 4H, 5G
The *Bouquinistes*, booksellers who set up their distinctive green stalls along the banks of the Seine, are a Paris institution. Besides used books (mainly in French), they also sell classic French posters and prints, even *fin-de-siècle* naughty postcards. Hours vary according to season and weather.

Madeleine & Rue du Faubourg-St-Honoré, 8th ❷ 2E/❸

The area surrounding La Madeleine is the shop window of classy Paris – much like Avenue Montaigne. Home to the really big names such as Hermès, Gucci, Ralph Lauren and Versace.

St-Germain-des-Prés to Montparnasse 6th, 14th ❷ 4E-6D

Wander along the boulevard. St-Germain lined with big name stores or you can lose yourself in the charming surrounding lanes amongst the numerous antique shops, fashion boutiques and bookshops.

St-Paul & L'Ile St-Louis, 4th ❷ 5H

Probably the prettiest area in the capital, the Ile St-Louis (see p.8) is like a tranquil village in the heart of the metropolis. You will find a diverse selection of well-presented small shops and galleries. Across the river Seine at 23-25 rue St-Paul there are a cluster of antique shops.

Department Stores

Printemps ❷ 1E

This huge store, built in the 1870s with an elaborate curved and colonnaded entrance has recently benefited from a revamp making its personal shopping service, with 12 languages spoken, second to none. For atmosphere alone, dine at the sixth-floor Brasserie, which sits below a huge stained-glass dome, 20 metres (66 feet) wide and 16 metres (53 feet) high. *64 boulevard Haussmann, T: 01 42 82 57 87. www.printemps.com*

BHV ❷ 4H

Each floor of this store offers a diverse selection of goods (white goods, lighting, stationery) but the Bazar de l'Hôtel de Ville is best known to Parisians as a place for the DIY enthusiast. *52-64 rue de Rivoli, T: 01 42 74 90 00, www.bhv.fr*

Bon Marché ❷ 5E

Designed by Gustave Eiffel and built in 1852, Le Bon Marché, Paris's oldest department store, is without

> **Opening Times**
> Most shops open 9/10am-7/8pm Mon-Sat, with the large department stores staying open until 9 or 10pm. Shops are often closed on Mondays and for up to 2 hours at lunchtimes. Some grocers and markets open on Sunday mornings as well as many shops in the Marais area.

The grand façade of Au Printemps

Shopping Areas

Bastille & Faubourg St-Antoine 4th, 11th, 12th ❶ 4H
This area is a favourite haunt of the Parisian youth. The streets are constantly buzzing with people perusing the boutiques.

Champs-Elysées & Av. Montaigne, 8th ❷ 1B, 2C
The Champs-Elysées is known for its eclectic array of designer shops, such as the flagship Louis Vuitton, upmarket automobile showrooms and pavement cafés. Equally Avenue Montaigne is known for its numerous *haute couture* and *prêt-a-porter*

The world-famous Shakespeare and Company

Window-shopping on the Champs-Elysées

designer boutiques.

Halles & Beaubourg, 4th ❷ 3G/❹
Home to a number of department stores such as BHV (*see p.17*) and the ugly 70s shopping mall, Forum des Halles. However, plans are well underway for a large-scale regeneration scheme (2008-13) that will transform the area under a canopy of glass, flooding it with light and hopefully turning it into a formidable shopping hub.

Latin Quarter, 5th ❷ 5F
This is the literary heart of Paris. The most famous of the many bookshops is Shakespeare and Company (❷ 5G), piled to the ceiling with titles new and old. *37 rue de la Bûcherie, T: 01 43 25 40 93, www.shakespeareco.org*

Le Marais, 4th ❶ 4G
Among the city's oldest areas, and home to the gay community, the Marais is a district of charming old streets with ancient stone buildings. More recently it has been christened 'Haut Marais' thanks to a migration of trendy designers into the area, increasing the concentration of small designer-boutiques and contemporary art galleries.

buy it places to shop

paris places to shop

Paris is the shopping centre of the world and the Parisians know it. They love to shop and their expeditions are not pastimes to be rushed but rather savoured and appreciated, in much the same way as they linger over their food. From the extravagantly expensive boulevards of the Champs-Elysées and the Montaigne to the tiny lanes of the Latin Quarter, Paris displays its formidable style. Even the department stores and arcades are regarded as monuments in their own right, with their vaulted galleries, glass ceilings and vast edifices. There is no better place to indulge in the reverence of retail worship than amongst the many colourful open-air markets where treasures of all kinds are waiting to be discovered.

Building Bridges

The flamboyant Pont Alexandre III, with its fantasia of cast-iron Art Deco lamp-posts and gilded statues, was built at the same time as the Grand Palais (see p.6) and the Petit Palais (see p.11) for the 1900 Universal Exhibition. It stretches in a single span of steel across the river Seine.

spared by the invading army. For a price – the loss of Alsace-Lorraine and a fine – the Prussians withdrew. And so this gleaming white basilica (with its amazing views over Paris) was completed in 1914; the interior, although always crowded, is a mass of soft red candle-light and exotic chapels. *Open 6am-11pm daily. Dome & crypt: Adm. Open daily 9am-6pm.*
35 rue de Chevalier de la Barre,
T: 01 53 41 89 00,
www.sacre-coeur-montmartre.com

Sainte-Chapelle ❷ 4G/❹

Louis IX commissioned this beautiful church to keep his collection of religious relics. Upstairs there are magical effects caused by the myriad stained-glass windows, particularly in the late afternoon as the sun shines through the rose window. *Open daily 9.30am-6pm Mar-Oct, 9am-5pm Nov-Feb. 4 boulevard du Palais,*
T: 01 53 40 60 97.

Tour Eiffel ❷ 4A

10,000 tonnes of iron held together by two-and-a-half million rivets go to make Paris's most famous landmark. Constructed by Gustave Eiffel for the 1889 Universal Exhibition, this soaring structure standing at 320 m (1,050 ft) remained the world's tallest building until the construction of the Empire State Building 40 years later. If you are feeling fit, climb the

The Tour Eiffel reaching into the sky

700 or so steps to the second-level Jules Verne restaurant, or take the lift all the way to the top from where, on a clear day, you can see for 80 km (50 miles). In summer it can take two hours to get to the top. *Adm. Open daily 9.30am-11.45pm Sep-Jun, 9am-00.45am Jun-Aug. Champ-de-Mars, T: 01 44 11 23 23,*
www.tour-eiffel.fr

Place de la Concorde

Winston Churchill, T: 01 53 43 40 00.
www.petitpalais.paris.fr

Place de la Bastille ❶ 4H

It was here that in July of 1789 the Parisian mob stormed the prison of the Bastille to release the inmates. The fact that there were only seven prisoners held at the time didn't bother the attackers; the jail was to them an emblem of the corrupt Royal state. Nothing now remains of the fortress. The 51.5-metre (169-ft) bronze *Colonne de Juillet* standing in the centre of the square was erected to the memory of the rebels who were killed in both the 1830 and 1848 revolutions. The square is the centre of national celebrations on Bastille Day, July 14 (*see p.60*).

Place de la Concorde ❷ 2D/❸

Originally named Place Louis XV, this square was the scene of more than 1,000 executions during the 1789 French Revolution – note the pink granite obelisk at its centre marking the spot where Louis XVI was beheaded. The biggest threat today comes not from the guillotine but from the maddening traffic that constantly roars around it.

Place Vendôme ❷ 2E/❸

It is surprising that this elegant square has remained intact, considering its troubled history. The first monument to grace the square was of Louis XIV on his horse, which was torn down by a revolutionary mob. Napoleon replaced it with a column made from cannons captured at Austerlitz, but that was destroyed by the communards in 1871. What stands here now is a column topped with a replica of Napoleon's statue, constructed three years later. The square is now home to the city's chicest jewellers and César Ritz's first hotel (*see p.55*).

Sacré Coeur ❶ 1F & inset ❶ 1G

In 1870 the Prussian army laid siege to Paris, cutting off all food supplies. Two wealthy Catholics decided to build a church if their city was renamed the Temple of Reason, but fell into disrepair. Restoration work began in 1841 and lasted 25 years. Inside don't miss the intricate stained-glass rose window. *Open 8am-6.45pm daily and until 7.15pm Sat & Sun. Place du Parvis-Notre-Dame, T: 01 42 34 56 10, www.cathedraledeparis.com*

Palais de Chaillot ❷ 3A

Across the river Seine from the Tour Eiffel stands the imposing Palais de Chaillot, aka Trocadéro. Built for the 1937 Great Exhibition, it reflected a new approach to neo-classical architecture on a massive scale. The area is the most museum-populated in the city, with several housed in the palais alone: **Musée National de la Marine**, *T: 01 53 06 69 53, www.musee-marine.fr*; **Musée de l'Homme**, *T: 01 44 05 72 72, www.mnhn.fr*; **the new Cité de l'Architecture et du Patrimoine**, *T: 01 58 51 52 00, www.citechaillot.org*; as well as the **Théâtre National de Chaillot**, *T: 01 53 65 30 00, www.theatre-chaillot.fr*

Rodin's 'The Thinker'

Panthéon ❷ 6G

So relieved was Louis XV to recover from illness in 1744 that he commissioned this vast church in thanks. Ironically he was long dead when it was completed in 1789, and revolutionary Paris was in no mood to be consecrating churches; in the 1790s it became a temple to the Revolution. It was reconsecrated twice but is now a state monument. Its dimly lit and peaceful interior houses the graves of Voltaire, Victor Hugo and Emile Zola as well as entrancing frescoes by Pierre Puvis de Chavannes. *Adm crypt. Open daily 10am-5.45pm Apr-Sep, 10am-5.15pm Oct-Mar. Place du Panthéon, T: 01 44 32 18 00.*

The serene dome of the Panthéon

Petit Palais ❷ 2D

Built along with the Grand Palais (*see p.6*), this beautiful pillared building is home to the Musée des Beaux-Arts, with its top-flight art collection. *Open 10am-6pm Tue-Sun. Avenue*

Notre-Dame in bloom

the 1970s, when it was saved by popular consent. It finally opened as a museum in 1986, and encompasses art and sculpture from 1848 to 1914 including the Impressionists. Don't miss Renoir's *Bal du moulin de la Galette*, Degas' ballerina statue and Monet's lilies. *Adm. Open 9.30am-6pm Tue-Sun, 9am-9.45pm Thu. 1 rue de la Légion d'Honneur, T: 01 40 49 48 14, www.musee-orsay.fr*

Musée Picasso ❶ 4G

The Hôtel Salé was converted in 1986 to house the vast amount of Picasso's art that was bequeathed to the state on his death in 1973. The collection covers the gamut of his changes in artistic style. The mansion retained its original 17th-century character when it was converted into the museum. *Adm. Open 9.30am-6pm Wed-Mon Apr-Sep; 9.30am-5.30pm Wed-Mon Oct-Mar. 5 rue Thorigny, T: 01 42 71 25 21, www.musee-picasso.fr*

Musée du Quai Branly ❷ 3B

This eccentric building designed by Jean Nouvel makes a controversial impact on the banks of the river Seine. Dedicated to the arts and civilisations of Africa, Oceania, Asia and the Americas, it contains some 300,000 exhibits, including sculptures, fabrics, statues and jewellery. *Open 11am-7am Tue, Wed, Sun; 11am-9pm Thu, Fri, Sat. 37 quai Branly, Portail Debilly, T: 01 56 61 70 00, www.quaibranly.fr*

Musée Rodin ❷ 4D

This 18th-century mansion contains many works by Rodin, the majority of which are marble or bronze sculptures. His two most famous works, *The Kiss* and *The Thinker*, can both be seen here. The rose garden is scattered with ornamental ponds and more of Rodin's sculptures, including studies for *The Burghers of Calais*. *Adm. Open 9.30am-5.45pm Tue-Sun Apr-Sep, 9.30am-4.45pm Oct-Mar. Hôtel Biron, 77 rue de Varenne, T: 01 44 18 61 10, www.musee-rodin.fr*

Notre-Dame ❷ 4H

This enormous church was started in 1163 when Pope Alexandre III laid the first stone, but it was 170 years and a couple of generations of architectural approaches later before completion. After the 1789 revolution the cathedral was vandalised and subsequently

Jardin des Tuileries ❷ 3E/❸

Stretching from the Louvre (see below) to the Place de la Concorde (see p.12), these very French 17th-century gardens once belonged to the old Palais Tuileries. In summer, a Ferris wheel provides great views of Paris, and the gardens are dotted with cafés, ponds and sculptures. *Open 7am- 9pm Apr-May & Sep, 7am-11pm Jun-Aug, 7.30am-7.30pm Oct-Mar. Tuileries, T: 01 40 20 90 43.*

Musée Carnavalet ❶ 4G

Made up of two mansions or *hôtels*, the Carnavalet depicts Paris's history, including whole rooms decorated and furnished in Renaissance style through to the stunning early 20th-century ballroom taken from the Hôtel de Wendel. *Open 10am-6pm Tue-Sun. 23 rue de Sévigné, T: 01 44 59 58 58.*

Musée du Louvre ❷ 3F/❸

The most famous work in the Louvre, which contains perhaps the greatest art collection ever found in one museum, is Leonardo da Vinci's *Mona Lisa*. The vast edifice was originally built as a fortress in the 12th century, remains of which can still be viewed within the building. Over the centuries it has been extended by successive kings, but no-one has changed it quite as radically as architect I M Pei did when he added the pyramid-shaped entrance to the courtyard in 1989. This museum is huge so get a floor-plan from the reception and choose what you want to see carefully. It's advisable to purchase your tickets in advance to avoid the lengthy queues (see box p.5). *Adm. Open 9am-6pm Thu & Sat-Mon, 9am-10pm Wed & Fri. Pyramide du Louvre, T: 01 40 20 53 17, www.louvre.fr*

Musée National du Moyen Age (Cluny) ❷ 5G

This 15th-century mansion is built on the ruins of Roman baths (see p.4), which are incorporated into the present building. The museum boasts medieval art and artefacts and the surrounding gardens replicate those of medieval times. *Adm. Open 9.15am-5.45pm Wed-Mon. 6 place Paul-Painlevé, T: 01 53 73 78 16, www.musee-moyenage.fr*

Musée d'Orsay from across the river Seine

Musée d'Orsay ❷ 3E

Situated on the Left Bank, this museum was originally a railway terminus built at the turn of the 20th century. The classic Beaux-Arts station closed for business in 1939 and was then threatened by the developers' bulldozer until

Cobbled courtyard of Musée Carnavalet

Ile St-Louis ❷ 5H

Unlike its larger neighbouring island (see p.7), Ile St-Louis remained as marshy grazing land until the 17th century, when it was drained and developed. It subsequently became popular with the Parisian middle classes. To live here is to have the most exclusive address in Paris.

Jardin du Luxembourg ❷ 5F

Whether you have been visiting the Panthéon (see p.11) or lunching in St-Germain, these gardens are an ideal place to relax amongst the many sculptures. They were originally laid out when the Palais du Luxembourg was built for Marie de Medici, widow of Henry IV, in the early 17th century, but were made grander in the 19th century. The gardens prove popular in summer with model sailing-boat hire on the pond, a puppet theatre for the kids and tennis courts. *Open daily 7.30am-9.30pm Apr-Oct, 8.15am-5pm Nov-Mar. Boulevard St-Michel, T: 01 42 34 25 95.*

Jardin du Palais-Royal ❷ 2F/❸

You can easily forget that you are in the centre of a busy city on entering these gardens. Surrounded by arcaded shops, galleries and cafés, they are a pleasant refuge from the bustle of Paris. *Open daily 8am-10pm Apr-May, 7am-11pm Jun-Aug, 7am-9.30pm Sep, 7am-8.30pm Oct-Mar. 6 rue de Montpensier, T: 01 47 03 92 16.*

Beautiful façade of the Musée du Louvre

Pont Alexandre III

event saw the building of the Grand Palais, the Petit Palais *(see p.11)* and the Pont Alexandre III bridge across the Seine *(see box, p.13)*. Thankfully the beautiful glass roof has been fully restored with the **Galeries Nationales** housing fantastic exhibitions in the west wing and the **Palais de la Découverte** with its Planetarium residing in the east wing. *(see p.58). Adm. Open 10am-8pm Mon, Thur-Sun, 10am-10pm Wed. Avenue Général Eisenhower, T: 01 44 13 17 17, www.rmn.fr*

Hôtel des Invalides ❷ 4C

The average 17th-century soldier, when invalided out of the army, had little option but to resort to begging on the street. Whether by an act of kindness or out of a desire to rid Paris of its legion of beggars, Louis XIV commissioned this hospice for his retired and disabled soldiers. Behind the magnificent façade is the **Musée de l'Armée**, which boasts an extensive warfare collection. In the centre of the complex lies the beautiful Dome Church, with its fantastic gilded roof. This church houses the remains of Napoleon Bonaparte, whose tomb now lies in the crypt. *Open daily 10am-6pm Apr-Sep; 10am-5pm daily Oct-Mar. 129 rue de Grenelle, T: 01 44 42 38 77, www.invalides.org*

Ile de la Cité ❷ 4G

The Celtic Parisii tribe settled on this picturesque island in about 250 BC. The Romans then invaded in 52 BC, pushing the Celts out and rebuilding and fortifying the tiny island. It remained the seat of French political power until the 14th century, when King Charles V moved his palace to the Louvre *(see p.9)*. In the 18th century, Baron Haussmann evicted all 'commoners' on the island out to the east of Paris and redeveloped the entire area. Today it is one of Paris's main tourist attractions, boasting **Sainte-Chapelle** *(see p.13)*, the **Conciergerie** and the **Palais de Justice** as well as **Notre-Dame** *(see p.10)* and a colourful flower market *(see p.19)*.

Dome Church, Hôtel des Invalides

see it

The striking Pompidou Centre

Apr-Sep. Place Charles de Gaulle, T: 01 55 37 73 77.

Bois de Boulogne ❶ 3A

Baron Haussmann designed this 900-hectare (2,224-acre) park in the west of Paris in the 19th century. Although an unwise destination at night, by day the park offers a wealth of activities including a children's amusement park, bike hire, boating on the lakes, horse-drawn carriage rides and even an open-air theatre where you can enjoy Shakespeare and a picnic come the summertime.

Centre Pompidou ❷ 3H/❹

Then-president Georges Pompidou commissioned the Pompidou Centre in 1960 to house the Musée National d'Art Moderne, arguably the most important modern art museum in Europe. Conduits, vents, escalators and other structures clutter the exterior of the building, which - unsightly to some, beautiful to others - incorporates clever design to maximise space for exhibition areas, an extensive public library, a cinema, shops and Le Georges top-floor restaurant *(see p.37)*. Open 11am-10pm Wed-Mon. Place Georges Pompidou, T: 01 44 78 12 33, www.centrepompidou.fr

La Défense Inset ❶ 1A

The French have always embraced new ideas, whether mechanical or architectural, and are happy to replace the old with the new. Evidence of this can be seen in the ultra-modern development of La Défense. Started in the 1950s, it has become one of France's major business centres, consisting of towering skyscrapers and impersonal walkways. Its crowning jewel is the Grande Arche: built to mark the bicentenary of the 1789 Revolution, this huge block, rising more than 110 metres (361 feet) above the ground, is big enough to fit Notre-Dame *(see p.10)* inside it. www.ladefense.fr

Grand Palais ❷ 2C

In 1900 Paris was basking in a period of peaceful content, a *Belle Époque* and decided to hold a second Universal Exhibition to show off the city's wealth. The

Tree-lined boulevard

a new generation of artists, writers and photographers settled in Montparnasse. *Ateliers* (studios) sprang up all over the place and the cafés buzzed with passionate debate. It was not to last; with the end of World War II, Paris emerged a more austere place, in which business and finance were considered more important than art. The giant Tour Montparnasse, an eyesore on the skyline, now dominates the area, but some of the *ateliers* and galleries remain. Of interest still is the cemetery where Jean-Paul Sartre, André Citroën and Serge Gainsbourg are buried. Boulevard Montparnasse offers a multitude of cafés and bars.

The Arc de Triomphe is at the confluence of 12 busy roads

Paris Museum Pass

It is worth taking advantage of this museum pass if you plan to visit a number of museums during your stay. The pass allows unlimited access to over 60 museums (permanent collections only) and monuments. You can purchase a two (€30), four (€45), or six (€60) day pass from participating museums and monuments, the CDG Airport, the Carrousel du Louvre Tourism Information stand and all the Paris Tourist Offices.

Sights

Arc de Triomphe ❷ 1A

The world's most famous triumphal arch stands majestically at the end of Avenue des Champs-Elysées. Napoleon Bonaparte commissioned the huge monument in 1805, following the army's victory at the Battle of Austerlitz, but due to setbacks, not least Napoleon's own fall from grace, the arch was not completed for 31 years. At 50 metres (164 feet) above ground, the viewing platform affords some of the best views of Paris. *Adm. Open daily 10am-10.30pm Oct-Mar; 10am-11pm*

Areas

Latin Quarter ❷ 5F
This area on the Left Bank of the Seine has a chequered past. The Romans settled it in 200 AD – evidence of this can be seen at baths in the Musée National du Moyen Age (see p.9) – and by the 12th century it was a great centre of learning, drawing scholars from all over Europe. By the Revolution in 1789, the area was run-down. Napoleon re-established a university at the Sorbonne as the mainstay of his educational reforms, breathing new life into the quartier and creating a hot-bed for the left-wing intellectuals who fuelled the uprisings of the 19th century. This was also the scene of student riots of 1968. The area, lively with cheap restaurants (of variable quality) serving students as well as tourists, retains its medieval charm.

Montmartre ❶ 1F & inset ❶ 1G
Bustling boulevards surround Montmartre, the highest point in Paris, just north of the city centre, but the surrounding side streets still evoke the village charm of an earlier era. The imposing Basilica of Sacré Coeur (see p.12) gazing down on Paris dominates the district. Tucked behind the church is the old artists' quarter, made famous by the likes of Matisse and Picasso, who lived and worked here prior to World War I, and more recently by the film *Moulin Rouge*. Inevitably, as the artists moved to less expensive dwellings in Montparnasse between the wars, the tourists moved in. Hundreds of souvenir shops, cafés and street artists (some of moderate talent) cater to the thousands of tourists, but the quartier has managed to hang on to its rather raffish and attractive air.

Montparnasse ❷ 6D
Between the two world wars, when the artists' quarter in Montmartre became too staid and too expensive,

Charming cobbled streets winding through Montmartre

see it places to see

paris places to see

From 250 BC, when the Celtic Parisii tribe settled on the Ile de la Cité, until the student demonstrations of 1968, Paris has endured a turbulent history of revolution, uprisings, occupancies and siege, forging her people into a resilient breed, and not one to be cowed by authority. The resulting city is one of a wealth of culture, architecture, fashion, the arts and gourmet food, all presented with the flamboyance that only Parisians can offer. From the beauty of Notre-Dame to the stark steel symmetry of the Tour Eiffel and the harsh boldness of the Grande Arche, Paris's broad avenues are packed with history, museums, galleries, shops, restaurants, cafés and bars to enhance your discovery of this great city.

CONTENTS

see it places to see	2
buy it places to shop	14
watch it places to be entertained	24
taste it places to eat and drink	34
know it practical information	44
directory hotel listings and more	54
speak it and index	62

Map references ❶ Le Grand Paris ❷ Centre de Paris
❸ Tuileries and Louvre ❹ Les Halles and Beaubourg ❺ Metro & RER